Land of Beginnings

Land of Beginnings

The Archaeology of Montana's First Peoples

Douglas H. MacDonald

MONTANA HISTORICAL SOCIETY PRESS
Helena

Front cover photograph: Jeremie Hollman.

Cover and book design by Luke Duran.

Printed in the United States.

Distributed by Farcountry Press, 2750 Broadwater Avenue, Helena, MT 59602
(800) 821-3874

ISBN 978-1-940527-03-1 (hardcover)
ISBN 978-1-940527-04-8 (ebook)

Library of Congress Cataloging-in-Publication Data available on request

I dedicate this book to my parents, Patricia A. Harlow and Richard C. MacDonald. They let me choose my own path. Both passed away during the writing of this book, but not before Dad could give me his comments on an early draft of the manuscript!

Contents

Acknowledgments

I have many people to thank for their help in the preparation of this book. Diana Di Stefano, the former editor-in-chief of the Montana Historical Society Press, was instrumental in the existence of the book. Cody Ewert of MTHS was extremely helpful in final editing. Monte White prepared all of the maps for the book. Many colleagues provided photographs for the book, including Stocky White, Dennis Jenkins, Bob Ackerman, Lauriane Bourgeon, Eske Willerslev, Ruth Gotthardt, Vladimir Pitulko, Ben Potter, Kathryn Krasinski, Patrick Rennie, Pete Bostrum, and Lbova Liudmila Valentinovna. Montana State University's Museum of the Rockies, the University of Montana's Mansfield Library, and the Montana Historical Society archives also granted permission to use images from their collections.

Thanks always to my family—Amy, Molly, and Otto—for their support during the writing of the book. Thanks also to my parents, Dick and Pat, and my wife's parents, Otto and Carol. Thanks to Barb, Rick, Shawn, and Declan for their care of mom and dad.

Finally, here's to all my colleagues and students who have worked with me on our archaeological projects across Montana and Wyoming for the last fifteen years. I've enjoyed every minute of the fieldwork, even as the snow fell in July in Yellowstone. Long live Two Oceanopolis and Squatch Holler!

Preface

When I was an undergraduate student, I spent a summer studying in central Mexico at la Universidad de las Américas in the city of Cholula. The largest pyramid in Mexico was a stone's throw from the university. As a long-distance runner, I used to run from campus up to the Spanish church on top of the pyramid for hill training. I tried to fend off the neighborhood dogs that would chase me through the streets around the pyramid with Spanish swear words. In their loose, well-worn khakis and wide-brimmed hats, the dogs' owners would watch me run by their adobe houses, awkwardly smiling at my invasion of their space on hot and dusty summer days. Runners like me put up with these conditions because the activity, as John Parker wrote in the book *Once a Runner*, serves as the only way to "marshal the ferocity of your ambition over the course of many days, weeks, months, and (if you could finally come to accept it) years. The Trial of Miles; Miles of Trials." Archaeology and running are similar endeavors: one requires lots of time spent on roads and trails, accumulating miles; the other involves lots of time spent troweling and digging in the dirt, accumulating history. Both tasks are arduous, sometimes requiring extreme levels of effort. But they are equally rewarding, contributing to participants' pursuit of happiness and their understanding of the human condition.

As I ran through the streets of Cholula, I saw bits of pottery and obsidian strewn around the pyramid and throughout the town. These artifacts marked the remains of the precolonial Indigenous cultures of Mexico. Mile after mile, I marveled at the history beneath my feet. At the time, I was studying international political economy and learning Spanish in anticipation of a career working for the World Bank or the International Monetary Fund. However, as I traveled around Mexico with several of my international student friends, I became interested in archaeology. We would catch the local buses and ride them to as close to the archaeological sites as we could get and then walk the rest of the way. Our visits to famous locales like Teotihuacan, Monte Alban, Xochicalco, Cacaxtla, and Cholula led me to take classes in archaeology when I returned to the United States. One of my undergraduate professors, Dr. Richard Gould, taught a class on hunter-gatherers. While I had always been interested in people, his course was inspirational because it made me think about the human past in a way that I never had before: we all were descended from hunter-gatherer ancestors. Lots of them.

Since that time, I've been studying the archaeology of hunter-gatherers. After all, if I was going to learn about the human condition, I figured I should study how we lived as humans for 99.9 percent of our history. Inspired by the amazing Paleoindian archaeology of Dr. George C. Frison, who taught at the University of Wyoming, my undergraduate honors thesis was a comparison of two Paleoindian archaeological sites in Wyoming. Those two sites—Horner and Mummy Cave—are on the banks of the Shoshone River, which winds its way eastward toward its confluence with the Bighorn River a few miles south of the Montana state line. Little did I know that I'd be writing a book about the first people of Montana more than thirty years after taking those initial steps toward a career in archaeology.

The study of the first Americans has interested me ever since I wrote my thesis and spent several weeks of 1990 in the hot sun and hard-packed earth of the Opuntia Meadows archaeological site, located north of Cody, Wyoming. Even though we didn't find a whole lot during our excavations, I became hooked on archaeology and the study of the past. As a doctoral student at Washington State University in the 1990s, my advisor William Andrefsky Jr. and my mentor Matthew J. Root hired me for an archaeological project near Killdeer, North Dakota. There, I met my wife, Amy Keil, and also found my dissertation topic: Native American hunter-gatherers of the Folsom period. Dated to more than ten thousand years ago, evidence of the Folsom culture has been unearthed at several archaeological sites across the Great Plains, including Montana, Wyoming, and the Dakotas.

Since finishing my dissertation on those 10,500-year-old Folsom sites in North Dakota, I have traveled around the United States and conducted archaeology in twenty states. While working across the country, my archaeology crews and I have found Clovis-age archaeological sites—which predate the Folsom culture—in four states, including Virginia, Pennsylvania, Wyoming, and Montana. The Clovis peoples have become known for their famous fluted points, such as the ones found at the Anzick site in Park County, Montana. I've conducted most of my archaeological research since I arrived as a professor at the University of Montana in 2006 in Yellowstone National Park. The two Yellowstone Clovis points our crew found in Wyoming and Montana, respectively, remain the only ones ever found within America's first national park.

I wish we had found more evidence of Clovis culture in Yellowstone. However, more than eleven thousand years ago, Clovis people largely avoided the high-elevation Yellowstone Plateau. After all, it was covered by three-hundred-foot-tall glaciers until just a few years before the first arrival of people. It was probably a mucky mess full of mosquitoes. As you can imagine, those first people to Yellowstone, Montana, and Wyoming preferred lower-elevation habitats, especially the vast grasslands that supported millions of large animals, including mammoths, horses, bison, and camels. Historian and retired University of Montana professor Dan Flores called this region an American Serengeti, comparing it to the expansive and rich grasslands of Africa. The original inhabitants of the land that would become Montana must have marveled at the wide-open spaces, so rich in wildlife but so lacking in people. This book tells their story. Their origins. Their travels from Asia. Their travels across snow and ice and oceans. Their lives as hunter-gatherers.

This book is a culmination of my three-decades-long obsession with the first peoples of the Americas. It attempts to answer several important questions: Where did they come from? Who were they? When did they arrive? How did they get here? The book is written for laypeople, including students of archaeology and those interested in the history of Montana and its Indigenous cultures. I hope that at least one of this book's readers is inspired to pursue archaeology as a career, to continue the quest to figure out the origins of Montana's first people, much as I was inspired by mentors like Richard Gould, Bill Andrefsky, Matthew Root, and George Frison, as well as by the pottery sherds and obsidian flakes that littered the streets as I ran up and down Cholula's great pyramid.

This is a fascinating story with many unanswered questions—we still have a lot to learn about Montana's first people: sites to find, dirt to dig, arduous work to be done. The trials of miles. Miles of trials.

CHAPTER ONE

The Indigenous Peoples of Montana

Who were the first Montanans? While this question is central to this book, the answer is relatively simple. The first Montanans were Native Americans, the Indigenous peoples of the place that later became the Big Sky State. The rest of the questions that this book asks are a little more difficult to answer: How long have Native Americans lived here? When did they arrive? Where did they come from?

Archaeologists like me have spent the last century working with Montana's first peoples to try to answer these questions. Despite these efforts, we still cannot fully answer them. Do we know where these people came from? Yes, we know they came from Asia, Siberia, and Alaska. But how exactly did they get here? Which route or routes did they take? When exactly did they make the journey? We know they made their way south at the end of the Late Pleistocene, sometime between twenty thousand and thirteen thousand years ago, but we are still not certain as to the precise timing of their original journey. While this book details what the archaeological data can tell us about this extraordinary migration, this chapter focuses on the state's Indigenous population.

Montana's Indigenous Tribes

The descendants of the first people to arrive in Montana belong to many Native American tribes, such as the Séliš (Salish), Ktunaxa (Kootenai), Piikuni (Blackfeet), Apsáalooke (Crow), Akaitikka (Northern Shoshone), Anishinaabe Ne-I-Yah-Wahk (Chippewa Cree), and Tsétsėhéstȧhase/Só-'Taeo'o (Northern Cheyenne), among others. Montana's tribes are independent nations with seven dedicated reservations in the state. Starting in the northeast portion of the state, Nakodas (Assiniboines), Lakotas, and Dakotas reside on the Fort Peck Indian Reservation. Slightly west, the Fort

A bison walks down a path in Yellowstone National Park in this 1941 Chris Schlechten photograph. Yellowstone's bison herd descends from animals that predate the arrival of humans to the Great Plains and Rocky Mountains over ten thousand years ago.
x80.6.2138, Museum of the Rockies, Bozeman

Belknap Reservation houses members of the Nakoda and A'a Ni Nin (White Clay) tribes. Rocky Boy's Indian Reservation, located on the Hi-Line (US Highway 2), is home to members of the Ojibwe and Anishinaabe tribes. Continuing west, the Blackfeet Indian Reservation of Montana is centered in Browning. To the southwest, the Flathead Reservation includes the Séliš, Kalispel (Pend d'Oreille), and Ktunaxa tribes. Near Great Falls, the Little Shell Tribe of Chippewa Indians of Montana received federal recognition in 2019 but lacks a dedicated reservation. Finally, in the far south-central portion of the state, the Apsáalooke and Tsétsėhéstȧhase/Só'Taeo'o people have two conjoining but independent reservations west of Billings.

Like the hundreds of tribal nations across the country, Montana's tribes are sovereign nations with independent governments, judicial systems, and law enforcement. The federal government consults with these tribes in what has been dubbed a government-to-government relationship. Even though many US laws had established this precedent, President Barack Obama signed an executive order into law in 2009 that required all federal agencies to consult with federally recognized tribes for any matter that might interest them. For example, I conduct much of my archaeological research in Yellowstone National Park, and any federal action in the park requires its superintendent and/or representative staff to consult with regional tribes, especially on matters of concern such as Yellowstone's famous bison herd. Bison have been an important food source for Montana's tribes for millennia. For that reason, the US government sought to eliminate bison in the late nineteenth century to upend the traditional subsistence means of Montana's tribes and force them to relocate to reservations and assimilate to the Euro-American lifestyle. As a result, Yellowstone's bison herd—descended from the original animals that lived in the region prior to the attempted decimation—is of profound importance to regional tribes. As per their federal responsibility, Yellowstone National Park consults with twenty-eight of those tribes on matters of cultural importance.

A Brief History Lesson

Prior to Euro-American contact in the early nineteenth century, more than a dozen Native American tribes hunted and gathered and lived their lives in Montana. In addition to the ten tribes with reservations in Montana, the Niimíipuu (Nez Perce) and Cáuigú (Kiowa) tribes, among others, were also active in this area. While Captains Meriwether Lewis and William Clark were among the first Euro-Americans to set foot in what became Montana in April 1805, they knew full well that many Indigenous people inhabited the area and had done so for a long time. In fact, Lewis and Clark relied on Native Americans, including several Nakoda women, to provide information on the mountains, rivers, and best routes for their trip through this unmapped territory.

Lewis and Clark were largely ignorant of and had little interest in the historical origins of the tribes they encountered in present-day Montana. However, at the time of that first contact, the tribes of Montana lived very much as they had been for at least twelve thousand years: as hunter-gatherers. They structured their society and lifeways around their need to move from place to place to find their food. They carried with them an enormous wealth of information about the region's wildlife, ecosystems, natural processes, and geology.

After Lewis and Clark and several other groups of Euro-American explorers launched expeditions of the West, the US government took a greater interest in the region. Following the discovery of gold in many areas of the West, and as boosters lauded the agricultural potential of the region, the government sought new ground for its growing population. In order to accommodate the nation's Manifest Destiny, as some at the time called the nation's need to expand toward the Pacific, the United States pushed west into space occupied by Indigenous cultures. To make room for American settlers, the US government resolved to place tribes on reservations, starting

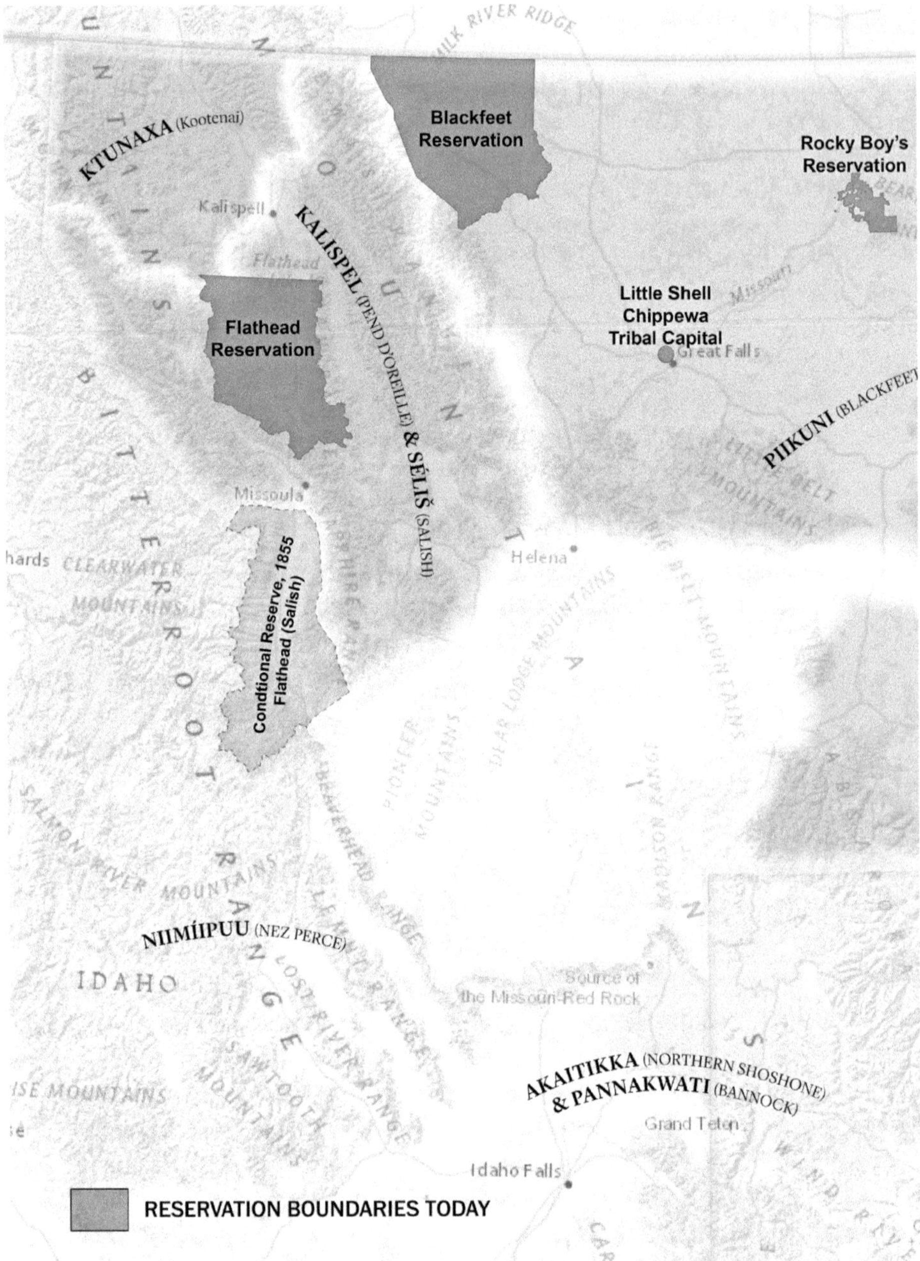

This map contrasts the traditional ranges of Native nations in present-day Montana and its vicinity with current reservation boundaries within the state. Monte White

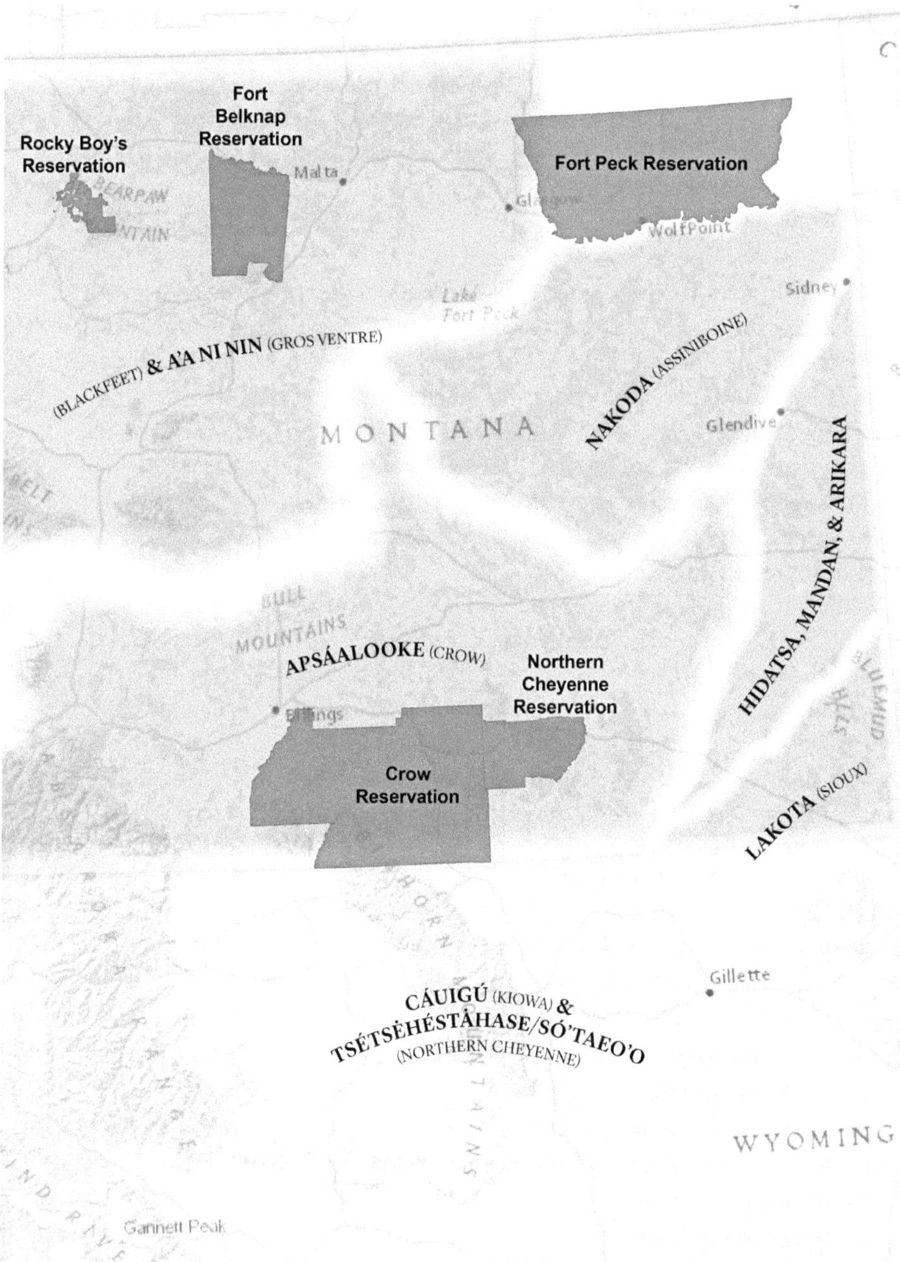

Fort Belknap Reservation
Rocky Boy's Reservation
Fort Peck Reservation
Malta
Glasgow
Wolf Point
Lake Fort Peck
Sidney
(BLACKFEET) & A'A NI NIN (GROS VENTRE)
NAKODA (ASSINIBOINE)
MONTANA
Glendive
HIDATSA, MANDAN, & ARIKARA
BULL MOUNTAINS
APSÁALOOKE (CROW)
Northern Cheyenne Reservation
Billings
Crow Reservation
LAKOTA (SIOUX)
Gillette
CÁUIGÚ (KIOWA) &
TSÉTSÈHÉSTÂHASE/SÓ'TAEO'O
(NORTHERN CHEYENNE)
WYOMING
Gannett Peak

in the 1850s. This attempt to isolate and assimilate Native peoples led to war with the Indigenous cultures of the Great Plains and Rocky Mountains, including many in Montana, who did not want to abandon their lands and lifeways. These groups had existed quite healthfully as hunter-gatherers since time immemorial: Why would they abandon their traditions?

The short answer is that the US government forced tribes to abandon that lifestyle through violent measures. The Lakota leader Sitting Bull led a coalition of Native warriors in the most famous of these Indian Wars, as so eloquently detailed in Megan Kate Nelson's 2021 book *Saving Yellowstone*. Sitting Bull was a member of the Hunkpapa Lakota tribe, who strongly resisted placement on reservations. US government pressure on the tribe sparked a war in which Sitting Bull led a group of Lakota warriors, with their Tsétsėhéstȧhase/Só'Taeo'o and Arapaho allies, against the US Cavalry at the famous Battle of Little Bighorn in 1876, just southeast of present-day Billings. Montana's Indigenous tribes call this fight the Battle of the Greasy Grass, the name of a tributary creek of the Little Bighorn River in southern Montana.

While Sitting Bull led the Lakotas and his united tribes to a decisive victory at Little Bighorn—including the killing of the famous US Seventh Cavalry leader George Armstrong Custer—their resounding triumph spurred an undaunted spate of revenge attacks by the US Cavalry. The most famous of these occurred in Montana Territory, as the great Niimíipuu leader Chief Joseph sought refuge in Saskatchewan, Canada, where Sitting Bull had fled earlier. In 1877, only one year after Sitting Bull's victory at Little Bighorn, Chief Joseph led more than seven hundred members of his tribe through Idaho, Wyoming, and Montana, including three days in Yellowstone National Park, which had been established in Indian Territory in 1872. The Niimíipuu hoped to avoid being placed on their government-defined reservation in Lapwai, Idaho. While the Niimíipuu weaved their way across lands settled by American colonists, they had battles and skirmishes with the US Cavalry. Ultimately, the cavalry stopped them within forty miles of Canada at the Battle of Bear Paw in north-central Montana.

While a couple hundred Niimíipuu under the leadership of White Bird escaped and made their way to Sitting Bull's encampment at Wood Mountain, Saskatchewan, US troops captured Chief Joseph and his band as prisoners of war. They never knew their hunter-gatherer lifestyle in the same way again. The Niimíipuu epitomize the fate of Indigenous people throughout the region. Neither Chief Joseph nor any of his band were allowed to return to their homeland in Idaho. After their capture at the Battle of Bear Paw, US troops first led the Niimíipuu to Oklahoma, then to the Colville Reservation in central Washington, where Chief Joseph was buried after his death in 1904. Today, the Colville Reservation, located alongside the Columbia River, is within sight of the Grand Coulee Dam, which the US Bureau of Reclamation constructed in the 1930s.

While Chief Joseph was captured in 1877, Sitting Bull remained in Saskatchewan. Along with White Bird's Niimíipuu, Sitting Bull led his united tribes on bison hunting trips into Montana Territory. Sitting Bull and White Bird sought allies among the Montana tribes to defeat the US Cavalry, making successful agreements with the Piikuni and Anishinaabe Ne-I-Yah-Wahk in northern Montana.

Sitting Bull eventually surrendered in the winter of 1880–1881. The annihilation of the bison herds had essentially exterminated Sitting Bull and his people's entire basis for subsistence. While White Bird fled further west into Canada, US troops took Sitting Bull and many other tribal members to Missouri as prisoners of war. Subsequently, federal officials moved the group to the Lakota reservation at Standing Rock, in present-day North Dakota, in 1883. Sitting Bull was killed by Indian agency police on December 15, 1890, over fears of an Indigenous uprising associated with the Ghost Dance religious movement. The US Army massacre of more than three hundred Lakota people at Wounded Knee occurred on December 29, just two weeks after Sitting Bull's murder.

The forced enculturation of the Plains and Rocky Mountain Indigenous peoples had dire consequences, including the loss of thousands of lives, as well as an unparalleled loss of Indigenous information built up over millennia: how to collect plants, animals, fish, and medicine; how to survive the wilderness; how to seek spirits and wisdom. Thousands of years of dedicated knowledge, practice, and prayer were nearly extinguished by a government convinced of its own Manifest Destiny.

The decimation of many aspects of Indigenous cultures was a travesty and one of the federal government's most despicable acts. This fact was acknowledged in a famous 2010 statement by US president Barack Obama, who apologized "on behalf of the people of the United States to all Native peoples for the many instances of violence, maltreatment, and neglect inflicted on Native peoples by citizens of the United States."

Indigenous Perspectives

One of the most amazing achievements of America's Indigenous peoples is their resilience in the face of subjugation. Many tribal members survived placement on reservations, language neglect, and forced enrollment in boarding schools, all with the goal of cultural assimilation to the American

Two Nakoda (Assiniboine) women in cloth dresses and shawls stand next to a tipi in this uncredited early twentieth-century photograph.

955-384, Montana Historical Society Photograph Archives

way. The remarkable endurance of North America's Indigenous communities continues to this day. Perhaps equally amazing is that modern tribal members can still help answer the many questions that scholars ask about the distant past. Many archaeologists seek information from contemporary Indigenous communities regarding their origins. While researchers have gathered a wealth of information on the origins of Montana's Indigenous tribes over a century of archaeological research, we still have a lot to learn, including the lessons Indigenous people have maintained over thousands of years through oral tradition.

Let's look at the remarkable narratives of two of Montana's Indigenous tribes to help determine answers to two major archaeological questions: When did they arrive in Montana, and how did they get here?

Piikuni Origins

In the early twentieth century, American anthropologists Clark Wissler and D. C. Duvall conducted interviews with many Piikuni individuals, ultimately writing their famous book *Mythology of the Blackfoot Indians* in 1908. Today, the term Blackfoot refers to the Blackfoot Confederacy, which includes three bands that reside mostly in Canada and the Piikuni, or Southern Piegan, formally known as the Blackfeet Nation of Montana. Wissler and Duvall conducted their research in north-central Montana among Indigenous people that had lived there for millennia. The first section of their book describes "The Making of the Earth." In this history, a great flood swept across the landscape. The flood was observed by Old Man, who sat on a high mountain with all the animals. Old Man sent a variety of animals, including otter, beaver, muskrat, and duck to collect earth, which they eventually found. It then rained, and everything grew. Old Man mixed the earth into its many colors and gave a cup of black water to the ancestors of the Blackfoot Confederacy—the Siksika (Blackfoot), Piikuni (Piegan), and the Kainai (Blood)—who spoke the same language. This drinking of the black water occurred on Chief Mountain, which is today the heart of the Blackfeet Indian Reservation in northern Montana.

Another story describes the movements of Old Man and Old Woman in their quest to "decide how the people shall live." Old Man, for instance, stated that women should tan hides using animal brains to make them soft and tools to scrape them. According to the story, Old Man and Old Woman also argued about many things, including whether people should live forever or only for a short time.

While these histories provide interesting perspective on the origins of Piikuni lifeways, another story collected by Wissler and Duvall describes the migration of people into north-central Montana and the Canadian provinces to the north. In this history, the first people lived on the other side of the ocean, and Old Man decided to move them to a better place. The story describes Old Man bringing the people across ice to the far north. As they moved, a boy who was riding on a dog travois saw a horn sticking through the ice. He cried because he wanted the horn, so his mother cut it off with an axe. As she cut

An unidentified Piikuni (Blackfeet) man rests on a tree in the mountains near Browning, Montana, in this early twentieth-century photograph. The stick he is holding includes an eagle feather and a scalp lock.

76.0353, Archives and Special Collections, Mansfield Library, University of Montana

the horn, the ice collapsed and only a portion of the people on one side of the ice continued to Piikuni country. Old Man was able to lead about thirty lodges of people across the ice, with each lodge holding one or more families.

These histories describe many aspects of Piikuni culture, but of most interest for this book is the migration story. Does this story tell of the earliest migrations from the north through the Ice-Free Corridor?

Séliš Origins

The tribes of far western Montana, including the Séliš, Ktunaxa, and Kalispel, are culturally related to tribes that live in the Columbia Plateau region of Washington, Oregon, and Idaho. This is due to the fact that all water in western Montana—west of the Continental Divide—flows into the Columbia River and the Pacific Ocean. For example, where I live in Missoula, Montana, the major rivers include the Blackfoot, Clark Fork, and Bitterroot, all of which eventually empty into the Columbia River and into the Pacific Ocean. So, while the Piikuni, as described above, have their origins to the north and east in the midwestern United States and Canada, western Montana tribes like the Séliš, Ktunaxa, and Kalispel are more closely related, speak similar languages, and share more cultural attributes with Indigenous people to the west. We should expect that their origin stories might also be different than those of the Piikuni. As we've seen, Piikuni origin histories describe travel across the ice—likely from the north and east—to get to their homeland in Montana.

For the Séliš, the story of Fish Man describes a possible western origin from the Pacific Coast toward the interior. The famous American anthropologist Franz Boas describes the Fish Man story in his book *Folk-Tales of Salishan and Sahaptin Tribes*, published in 1917. Another important anthropologist, James Teit, collected this same history during his anthropological research among the interior Séliš tribes of British Columbia that live along the Fraser River. The story describes the journey of a girl to the coast during a time when all the interior rivers dried up and the fish died. When the girl reached the sea, she saw that the people there made their houses of wood planks covered with mats and blankets. Eventually, the seas rose and transported the girl and her lover back to her home in the interior, bringing with them many fish. They instructed the people to live in the wood plank houses and told them that they would have plenty of fish and plenty of food.

Does this indicate a Pacific coastal origin for the Séliš people of Montana and its vicinity? If so, this history may also lend credence to the idea that Montana's first peoples migrated along the Pacific Coast before moving into the interior.

Conclusion: Indigenous Perspectives

Anthropological, archaeological, and Indigenous perspectives are not mutually exclusive. Each can be beneficial to better understanding humanity and its diverse cultures. While archaeologists have not always taken Native American viewpoints into consideration in their research, they have attempted to improve these relationships in recent years, with the ultimate goal being an enhanced historical accounting. There have also been numerous federal, state, and tribal laws passed in the last fifty years or so that have required archaeologists working with Native American remains to take tribal ownership and perspectives into account. Among these is the 1990 Native American Graves Protection and Repatriation Act (NAGPRA), which provides protections for Indigenous human remains and demands that federally funded museums return culturally important items to tribes.

Today, archaeologists strive to incorporate Indigenous viewpoints in their accounts of pre-contact history. As described above, Piikuni history describes migration across the ice to their homeland in the eastern front of the northern Rocky Mountains and the northern Great Plains, including Montana. This makes sense given that we know they derive from cultures that lived further north and east in southern Canada and in the upper Midwest. Eventually, perhaps a few thousand years ago, they migrated west to Montana. Their origin stories, however, speak of crossing the ice to their homeland, possibly implying that their original ancestors marched south through the Ice-Free Corridor. Or do these stories simply imply that the Piikuni people migrated to Montana more recently—three thousand years ago or so—from the midwestern United States and that their journey took them across snow and ice?

Similarly, the origin story of the Séliš in interior British Columbia describes the movement of fish-adapted cultures from the Pacific Coast to the interior. Does this describe the origin of those people in their journey from the Pacific Coast through interior river valleys at the end of the Last Glacial Maximum, more than twelve thousand years ago? Or is it the history of a more recent journey, one depicting the movement of people from the coast to the interior, that occurred frequently for the Séliš-speaking cultures of the interior regions of North America? Perhaps it describes both.

These two distinctive histories of the Piikuni and Séliš people support the archaeological data in that they accurately describe tribal origins and the regions they are associated with, including the interior of North America for the Piikunis and the coast of North America for the Séliš. Is it possible that interior tribes such as the Piikunis are the descendants of people that migrated south through the Ice-Free Corridor into Canada and interior

North America twelve thousand years ago? Is it also possible that the tribes of far western Montana are the descendants of people that migrated east from the Pacific Coast even earlier? I'd say that it is absolutely possible.

The remainder of this book looks at archaeological findings that can help us understand the origins of Montana's Indigenous peoples. *Land of Beginnings* focuses on Clovis and potential pre-Clovis sites in Montana and the surrounding region, but it does not address notable Folsom sites such as MacHaffie and Indian Creek, both near Helena, or Goshen sites such as Mill Iron in southeast Montana, all of which are covered in greater detail in my 2012 book *Montana Before History*. While Native peoples' forced placement on reservations and the near decimation of their populations led to a loss of much Indigenous knowledge, tribal scholars and archaeologists have led a renewed effort to find their origins and help tribes understand their history and how they came to places like Montana and the rest of the lands we now know as the United States of America.

✷

CHAPTER TWO

How Can Archaeology Help Us Understand?

Thousands of hours of archaeological research have been conducted in Montana and the surrounding region to try to explain how and when humans first arrived there. Similar investigations have taken place throughout the western hemisphere. Indeed, more research exists on Native American origins than any other topic in American archaeology. Since the nineteenth century, and particularly after archaeologists excavated Clovis projectile points from the ribs of mammoths in New Mexico in the early twentieth century, historians and archaeologists have sought to understand how people came to the Americas.

Even with all that research, do archaeologists know who were the first people to come here and when they arrived? Just how long have Native Americans been in Montana, the Rocky Mountains, and the Great Plains? It's an exciting question. When I visit the Yellowstone River valley and other areas of Montana and Wyoming to conduct my research, my goal is to discover artifacts and features at archaeological sites, evidence of people and where they lived, that date back thousands of years. These artifacts include stone tools, projectile points, pottery, animal bones, and plant remains. Features include evidence of fire pits, such as one in Yellowstone that was used to cook plants, as well as living structures and other types of activity areas where people conducted routine tasks. My University of Montana students and I find amazing discoveries associated with Montana's earliest inhabitants almost every day during our summer field season. From stone circles that mark the locations of Native American lodges, to debris from the production of obsidian tools, to handprints left on rock faces, we find evidence everywhere we look.

Along with dozens of other archaeologists in Montana, our work at archaeological sites aims to help solve the questions of when and how Native

Americans first arrived in this region. But despite all this archaeological research, which includes excavating dozens of sites that contain thousands of artifacts, we still cannot be certain as to the precise date when humans first entered Montana. Until recently, we had the date range narrowed down to a four-thousand-year window, between eleven thousand and fifteen thousand years ago.

However, in the late 2000s, archaeologists working at White Sands National Park in the Tularosa Basin of south-central New Mexico uncovered footprints left by now-extinct mammals, including giant sloths, camels, and mammoths. These animals disappeared at the end of the Late Pleistocene, so archaeologists immediately knew that the footprints were at least twelve thousand to thirteen thousand years old. While archaeologists knew that humans lived in North America at that time, they thought this period was around when they first arrived on the continent. So, without a doubt, the discovery of human footprints side-by-side with these extinct mammals was one of the most remarkable archaeological finds of the early twenty-first century.

Even more amazing, White Sands National Park archaeologist David Bustos and his Bournemouth University colleague Matthew Bennett

In 2021, researchers from the University of Montana—including Caleb Sobczak (left), Kyler Mozell (center), and the author (right)—excavated this Native American fire pit, which dates to about 250 years ago, near the Gallatin River in Yellowstone National Park. Soil analysis revealed that the pit was used to cook wild plants. Bradan Tobin photograph

recognized the presence of carbonized seeds within and below the footprints. The seeds were identified as being from the *Ruppia cirrhosa* plant, commonly known as spiral ditchgrass. The plant has grown in the marshy areas near the deserts of the American Southwest for tens of thousands of years. Since the seeds are organic, the team was able to radiocarbon-date them to twenty-three thousand years ago. Given that the seeds were both below and within the footprints implies that humans walked on the same ground at about the same time. Thus, these footprints—one group of which indicate that a hunter walked behind and stalked a giant sloth—show the likelihood that people were present in New Mexico more than twenty thousand years ago. Given that the sites previously thought to be the oldest in North America date to a bit more than twelve to fourteen thousand years ago, the White Sands footprints indicate a human presence far earlier than archaeologists previously thought.

As with so many other ancient Native American archaeological sites, however, the dates of the White Sands footprints have come under scrutiny. The most recent studies, published in the journal *Quaternary Research* in 2023, have shown reason for pause before accepting these dates. The authors of the critique—Charles Oviatt, David Madsen, David Rhode, and Loren Davis—state that since the plant grows in water, it might be subject to something called the reservoir effect, which produces anomalously old radiocarbon dates. While this most commonly occurs with organic materials from maritime environments, it means that the footprints from White Sands might not be as old as originally thought. In fact, the authors radiocarbon-dated modern seeds from the same plant—known to have been collected for a museum in 1947—to around six thousand years ago. These data suggest that the White Sands footprints might be only twelve thousand or thirteen thousand years old.

While the White Sands footprints may only date to the Late Pleistocene, they still clearly show that early Native Americans lived side-by-side with now-extinct mammals. The newest data seem to substantiate the hypothesis that people resided in the southwestern deserts of North America earlier than many other places in the continent. Although the earliest dates attributed to the White Sands footprints have been potentially discredited, the site still stands as one of the few in the western United States to show reliable evidence of early Native Americans coexisting with these animals.

While the question of when the first humans arrived in North America remains a subject of debate, as the White Sands example makes clear, we know that the first Montanans came from Asia and that they were most definitely hunter-gatherers. This is an indisputable fact. Montana's first peoples lived off the resources provided by their environment. They gathered plants such as bitterroot, camas, and pine nuts in the mountains and plains. They hunted mammoth, bison, elk, and horses in the open grasslands and foothills. They fished for salmon and trout in the lakes, rivers, and creeks. They collected rock at numerous quarry locations to make stone tools.

In other words, they knew the landscape in an intimate fashion that allowed them to survive. Humans have lived everywhere on earth, with the exception of Antarctica, for a very long time, surviving and thriving by adapting to new worlds through technological innovation and human ingenuity. One thing that anthropology—the study of people—has taught me is that humans will do whatever it takes to adapt and survive. The emergence of human cultures—so varied yet so similar—is a result of our adaptiveness, our ability to use earth's resources to survive in any climate and any region.

While it is an indisputable fact that the first Montanans were hunter-gatherers, the Indigenous tribes in this region were not unique in this respect. Today, while most of us go to grocery stores and restaurants for our subsistence, 99.9 percent of our human ancestry is linked to people that hunted, gathered, and fished for their day-to-day subsistence. It's hard to fathom that our current world of cell phones, satellite television, the internet, and other advances of modern technology is an anomaly—a blip on the radar—in our long history on the planet.

Ancient Origins and Migrations

To better understand the first Indigenous hunter-gatherers to live in Montana, it is important to understand human origins in deep time. The earliest human ancestors evolved in Africa as hunter-gatherers more than one hundred thousand years ago. Much as people do today, they moved around in order to survive. For instance, I've lived all over the United States, moving to different places to find income to be able to buy food and provide shelter for my family. Of course, I used planes, trains, and automobiles to facilitate this travel. While our hunter-gatherer ancestors were also mobile, they did not have any mode of transportation other than their own feet. Many had dogs that helped transport their tools, food, and shelter, likely using travois (sleds) built from long wood poles. They probably also carried gear in large leather and textile packs attached to the dogs and to their own backs. But since they carried the items that they needed with them at all times, they had to make an extreme effort to minimize travel weight.

About one hundred thousand years ago, the earliest humans moved out of Africa and into the Middle East, to places like present-day Israel and Iraq. Not simply looking for new locales to occupy, they were expanding their

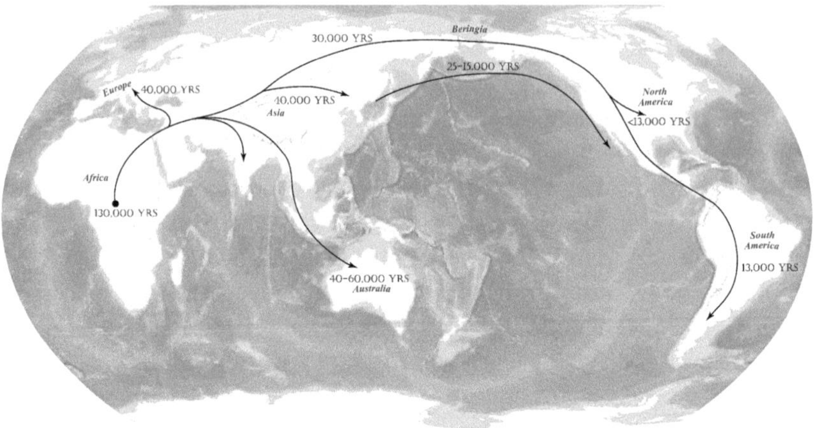

People first migrated to North and South America sometime prior to thirteen thousand years ago, as this map charting how human populations have dispersed over time shows.
Monte White

known territories to increase their odds of survival and to have more food and resources. This mode of travel eventually led them into Europe and Asia about fifty thousand years ago, if not earlier. In fact, there is evidence that these earliest people even made it to Australia by that time, meaning that early humans had developed the maritime technology that was required to cross the oceans from southeast Asia.

In ancient Europe, at places like the famous archaeological site of Dolni Vestonice in the Czech Republic, early hunter-gatherers intensively harvested large animals, even using mammoth bones to build a fence around their village nearly thirty thousand years ago. People eventually pushed even further north into the sub-Arctic and Arctic regions of Asia and Europe, developing advanced technologies for clothing and shelter that allowed them to live in very cold climates. People also continued to move north up the Pacific Coast of Asia, making it to the northern regions of Japan and Kamchatka by around forty thousand years ago or so.

One of the earliest indications of people in interior northeastern Asia dates to about twenty-four thousand years ago at the Mal'ta site near Lake Baikal in eastern Russia. These hunter-gatherers pushed even further north to the edge of the Arctic Circle. One of the earliest sites in this region is the Yana Rhinoceros Horn site (RHS). Archaeological excavations at this site revealed that the earliest humans in northeastern Russia hunted now-extinct mammoths and rhinoceros as early as twenty-seven thousand years ago. They lived within a day's journey by foot of the Arctic Ocean. While interior-adapted hunter-gatherers hunted large megafauna along the major interior rivers and plains of Russia, the earliest archaeological sites in Japan and coastal northeastern Asia show a maritime adaptation in which people traversed the coast in kayaks while fishing and hunting for subsistence.

The early hunter-gatherers who migrated to eastern and northeastern Asia and eventually made it to North America were subsistence hunters and fishers. But which of these groups made it to Montana first? Did the early settlers of coastal northeastern Asia migrate around the coast of the Pacific, or did the interior people of Siberia continue inland into the Americas?

Amazingly, we can connect these earliest people in Asia directly to the ancestors of the first Montanans. DNA studies of human genetics show an ancient link between people living in Montana eleven thousand years ago and people living at Lake Baikal twenty-four thousand years ago. The lifestyles of the people living at Yana RHS near the Arctic Circle are also quite similar to those found at the earliest sites in North America. In both Russia and Montana, these people hunted large animals, including mammoths, to make a living. At the same time, the people living on the Pacific Coast of the Americas were clearly descendants of migrants from coastal Asia. So, when we say that we know who the first Montanans were, we can clarify that they were Native Americans who lived a hunter-gatherer lifestyle and that they came from northeast Asia.

The Role of Archaeology in Understanding the First Montanans

I have been digging up evidence of human activities across North America for over thirty years. I've conducted archaeological excavations in twenty states—from Pennsylvania and Kentucky to North Dakota, Montana, and Wyoming—trying to find evidence of the first people. In these archaeological expeditions, no matter where I've worked, my teams and I have looked for sites in the same way while hunting for similar types of artifacts and features. We can do so because Native American hunter-gatherers, living off both the land and the sea, have occupied every nook and cranny of North America. My goal during an archaeological expedition is to find these sites, the places where people lived in the past.

How do we find archaeological sites? Isn't it a bit like finding a needle in a haystack? It sometimes seems that way, but we have practices that help us locate these ancient camps and villages. We typically use two methods to find archaeological sites: surface survey and shovel test pit excavation. Surface survey entails archaeologists walking the ground surface in areas where people would have lived in the past. The most common locations for archaeological sites are near water or other resources useful for hunter-gatherers' survival. Basically, any place that you or I might consider a good camping spot, so did early Native Americans. So, in places like the Clark Fork River valley of western Montana, my teams often walk along a river terrace to find artifacts and features that mark a place where people lived in the past. We find mostly stone tools, which were the predominant means of survival for early Montanans.

I often remark that the first Montanans were the original hard-rock miners. What I mean is that the earliest hunter-gatherers quickly found outcrops of rock suitable for producing stone tools. Not every rock is useful for stone tool production. The key is a high degree of silica (or glass) content in the rock. Native Americans commonly collected obsidian—or volcanic glass—to make tools because it is comprised of nearly 100 percent silica. That makes it among the sharpest natural substances on earth. This is true not just in Montana and the Rocky Mountains but also in Japan, Alaska, and Siberia, or any area where volcanism released magma that cooled quickly and with a high enough silica content to make obsidian. The extreme sharpness of the volcanic glass made it an ideal material for hunter-gatherers. They mined the rock to make stone tools with which they could kill and eat animals and collect and process plants. One of the obsidian quarries in Yellowstone has nearly one hundred large pits excavated by Native Americans over the last eleven thousand years to collect volcanic glass to make stone tools. There are similar rock quarries all over Montana, locations where Native Americans mined for rock for thousands of years.

Chert is also common throughout the Rocky Mountains. In contrast with obsidian, which forms due to volcanic activity, chert forms in the sedimentary layers of the earth, especially in limestone formations, which often are high in silica. Even before arriving in this region, humans understood this material and knew the geological formations in which to find it. It is not surprising, then, that Montana's first peoples searched not only for the best places to hunt animals and collect plants but also for the best places to collect stone, such as volcanic calderas (obsidian) and limestone formations (chert). They looked for these places and excavated rock from the earth in vast quantities. Imagine hundreds of generations of Native American families excavating pits in the rock formations for thousands of years. Obsidian Cliff in Yellowstone is estimated to have enough obsidian to fill three thousand football stadiums. Another quarry near Anaconda revealed dozens of deep pits that Native Americans excavated into the bedrock to collect the local mustard-yellow chert for stone tool production.

Thousands of years of stone tool production in Montana has resulted in some very large rock quarries; this is why the earliest Native Americans were Montana's first hard-rock miners. Native American hunter-gatherers didn't just casually collect the rock, they purposefully found the best locations and excavated large amounts of it for use in their daily lives, leaving behind deep quarry pits and evidence of stone tool manufacture. Dozens of similar locations across Montana reveal that the first Montanans found these outcrops of rock quite early, within a generation or two of their arrival. They must have actively looked for these rock outcrops to ensure their survival.

Evidence of stone tool manufacture such as black chert flakes are a ubiquitous presence at Montana archaeological sites. While some sites have just a few stone artifacts, other sites contain millions of fragments of stone tools, evidence that Native Americans actively used that location for thousands of years. This is not to say that other types of materials—such as bone, antler, ivory, wood, shell, or leather—weren't useful, but that those materials don't preserve as well in the archaeological record. Soil at archaeological sites

A University of Montana researcher holds a large cobble of obsidian from a quarry in Yellowstone National Park near West Yellowstone, Montana. Native Americans collected obsidian to make stone tools. Author photograph

often degrades organic materials quickly, leaving behind only stone artifacts, meaning these tools often provide the only remaining signs of the earliest Montanans. To be sure, these people produced other types of tools from organic materials, including hunting implements, butchering tools, and clothing. A few sites in Montana, including the famous Pictograph Cave in Billings, have preserved a broader array of organic materials due to their dry conditions. At that site, archaeologists found well-preserved textiles produced from plant fibers and bone from numerous animals and humans.

Another way to find archaeological sites is to dig holes. I am very good at digging square and round holes. If my career as an archaeologist ends, I could go to work on a ranch digging postholes for fences. Archaeologists dig to find sites that might be buried beneath the earth or are otherwise difficult to see on the ground surface. For example, some areas on the landscape have lots of dense vegetation in which the surface of the ground is invisible. In this type of landscape, we would dig round holes at equal intervals—say every fifty feet—to try to find artifacts and sites. Once we find sites, we investigate them more intensively to try to figure out their age of use and their purpose, or why people lived there. At one site in Yellowstone, we conducted systematic excavations and found abundant evidence that Native American hunter-gatherers lived at the site. During that excavation, we collected all of the artifacts that we sifted through mesh screens and analyzed them at our lab at the University of Montana.

Archaeologists use these same methods everywhere that they look for evidence of early people. Some methods are more advanced, such as ground-penetrating radar or magnetometry, which allow the archaeologist to see evidence of human activity below the ground without digging. My colleagues use these subsurface imaging technologies when possible, as do most archaeologists. The ultimate goal is to find the locations where the earliest people lived in Montana and elsewhere. Our aim is to trace human movements around the globe by looking at the items they left behind in different locations.

Another important aspect of modern archaeology is the ability to place a date on artifacts and sites that we find during an expedition. Archaeologists have two ways of establishing chronologies for artifacts, sites, and cultures. The first is by radiocarbon dating, in which ten-thousand-year-old organic materials found at archaeological sites can be precisely dated within thirty to fifty years of the day from which a person used them. The age of an organic artifact can be dated by measuring the amount of the element carbon-14 present in an organic artifact. Carbon-14 has a known half-life and a known rate of decay, and by measuring the amount of it in an organic material, archaeologists can determine when an organism died, revealing the age of the artifact. The most common type of organic material found at sites is charcoal or burned wood. Hunter-gatherers built fires all over the world in order to cook food and stay warm, especially in cold places like Montana. For instance, our University of Montana team excavated a hearth feature in Yellowstone that Native American hunter-gatherers used thousands of years ago. I always look for evidence of these fires at archaeological sites so that I can find charcoal, which will allow my team to place an age on the site. Other types of commonly dated organic artifacts at sites include bone, antler, wood, ivory, plants, and even hair.

There are two types of dates associated with radiocarbon dating: first, the radiocarbon dates; and second, their calibrations. While I choose to use the actual radiocarbon dates in years before present (BP) in this book, many archaeologists have switched to the use of calibrated dates. The latter form renders the radiocarbon dates equivalent to our modern calendar years, more or less. For the period of study in this book, the Late Pleistocene epoch, the calibrations typically are about two thousand years older than the actual radiocarbon dates. The calibrations are always changing as well, as they are refined in comparison to tree ring chronologies and the like. For example, the radiocarbon age for the Anzick site, Montana's most important (and oldest) archaeological site, is 11,000 years BP. The calibration date, in contrast, is about 12,800 calendar years ago.

Another way to date an archaeological site is to analyze the types of artifacts found during excavations. Many artifacts, including projectile points and pottery, for example, have diagnostic styles that allow archaeologists to place an age on them. For example, Anzick is a Clovis site. We have radiocarbon dates that tell us it is eleven thousand years old. We also have Clovis-style projectile points that have diagnostic attributes unique to Clovis technology. If you find a Clovis projectile point, that means an early hunter-gatherer lived there eleven thousand years ago. No other human culture in the Americas or Asia produced these types of projectile points. Without these types of diagnostic artifacts, it would be much more difficult for archaeologists to determine the ages of sites, since many of them don't yield organic materials, such as charcoal, that can be dated by the radiocarbon method.

While this book is about archaeology, it is more about the results of those efforts than the methods of investigation and analysis. The rest of the book will examine the results of the archaeological projects that have yielded evidence of the first people in Montana. That information will help us better construct the story of the first Montanans beyond what we already know,

Indigenous hunters used Clovis points, such as this one from the Colby site in Wyoming, to kill mammoths, horses, and camels more than eleven thousand years ago across North America.

Artifact courtesy of Lithics Casting Lab. Author photograph

including approximately when they arrived in Montana, how they got here, how and where they lived, the types of tools they used, and even how they went about their daily lives.

✷

CHAPTER THREE

Where Did the First Montanans Come From?

There was much controversy about the origins of the earliest Montanans until February 2014. That month, the scientific journal *Nature* published an article by Eske Willerslev, Sarah Anzick, and a slew of coauthors, including one of my own doctoral students from the University of Montana, Samuel "Stocky" White. The article announced the findings of genetic research of an ancient skeleton found at the Anzick site near Wilsall, Montana, in the 1960s. While the eleven-thousand-year-old human remains had been found nearly fifty years earlier, genetic research was not possible due to their poor condition. By the late 2000s, however, technological advances allowed for the analysis of poorly preserved remains. So, the results of the Anzick genetic research were among the most important ever announced for an archaeological site in Montana.

The news media jumped on the findings as some of the most significant in the history of North American archaeology. The popular magazine *Science* laid out the details of the article under the title "Native Americans Descend from Montana Boy." The Montana boy they referred to was now a set of ancient remains—a skull and a few other bone fragments—at the Anzick site. I dedicate an entire chapter to Anzick, unquestionably Montana's most important archaeological site, later in this book, but it is important to highlight its contributions to our understanding of the origins of Montana's Native Americans now because it provides evidence of a genetic link between this region's Indigenous peoples and their ancestors in northeast Asia and Siberia.

Genetic studies of ancient human remains have solved numerous archaeological mysteries in recent years. The Anzick study is just one of numerous similar genetic studies by Eske Willerslev and his colleagues. Their research, among others, has provided insight into human origins by

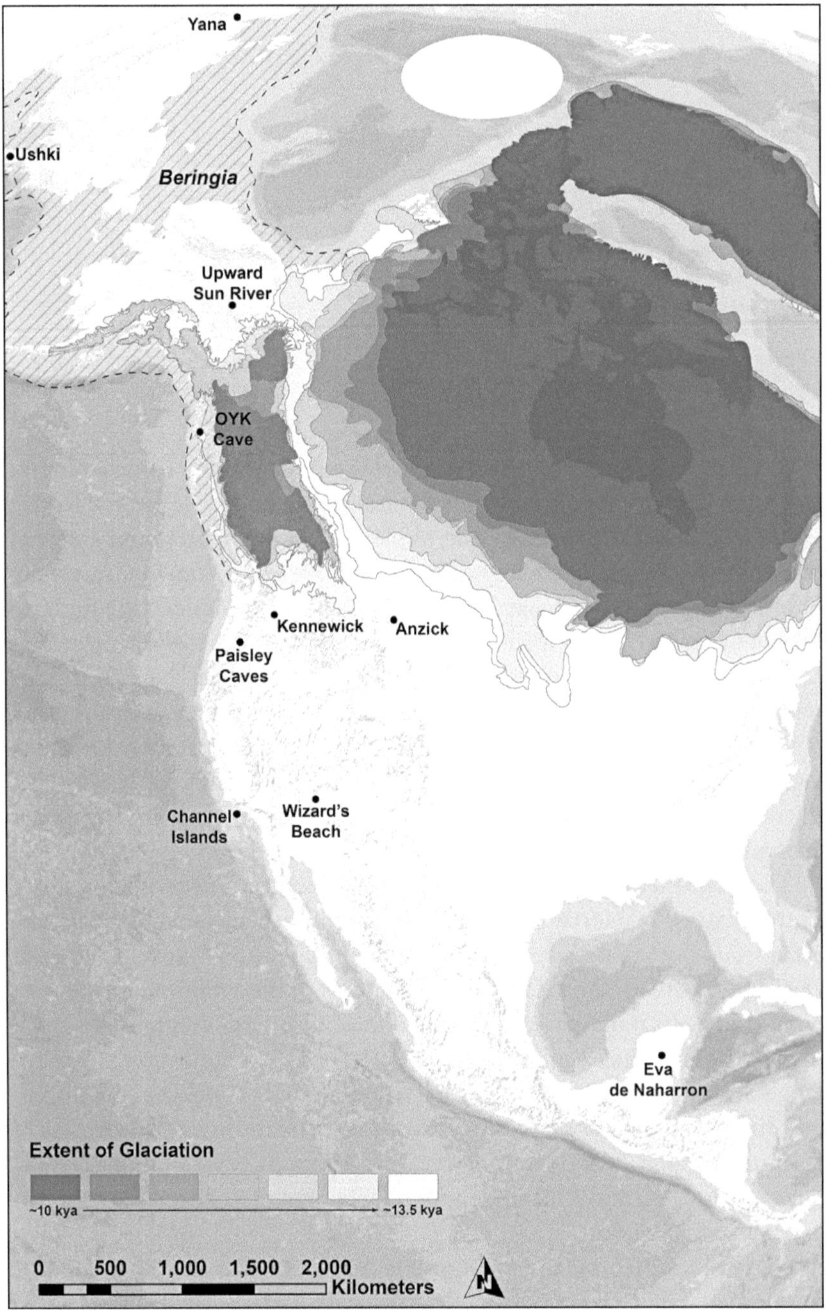

This map shows North American Paleoindian archaeological sites that have yielded human remains. Monte White

linking genetic research to archaeological sites all over the world. Genetic research continues to answer important questions involving human origins, including the ones surrounding the first Montanans.

I first heard Eske Willerslev speak at a public lecture he gave at the University of Montana in Missoula in 2013, during which he presented the preliminary results of his Anzick boy research. I remember him being so thrilled by the findings of the study that he could barely contain himself. His excitement was contagious, and many of us walked away from the lecture thinking we were one step closer to solving the mysteries of the first Americans.

Willerslev is a professor of ecology and evolution at the University of Cambridge in London and serves in a similar role at the University of Copenhagen in Denmark. His team's genetic research has revolutionized the study of the first Americans, and his lab has studied the genetic relatedness of humans across the globe. Born in 1971, Willerslev grew up in Denmark and attended the University of Copenhagen, studying genetics while his twin brother studied anthropology. The twins' father, a historian, spurred their interest in ancient history, leading them to conduct several archaeological and anthropological expeditions to Siberia in their early years of scientific inquiry. It should be no surprise that Willerslev's research led him to study the first Americans given that archaeological research had indicated for more than a century that the earliest Native Americans likely traveled from Asia and Siberia more than eleven thousand years ago.

A Solutrean-Clovis Connection?

So, if the prevailing archaeological theory for most of the twentieth century was that Native Americans were of Asian origin, why was Willerslev and his colleagues' genetic research on the Anzick boy so important? Didn't this DNA study tell us something we already knew? Well, sort of. Their study proved serendipitous because it followed the emergence of an alternative hypothesis that the first Americans came from Europe.

Dennis Stanford of the Smithsonian Institution and renowned stone tool technology researcher Bruce Bradley proffered what they called the Solutrean hypothesis in 2004. Bradley identified several similarities between the stone tools of Solutrean Europeans of seventeen thousand years ago and those used by Clovis, one of the earliest cultures of the Americas. Based on these similarities, Bradley proposed that Clovis culture descended directly from the Solutreans. Dennis Stanford joined him in suggesting that the eleven-thousand-year-old Clovis culture had European rather than Asian origins. Now there were two archaeological hypotheses to explain the first Americans. This meant that the human remains found at Anzick were of extreme importance to solving the first Americans mystery.

Stanford and Bradley proposed that maritime-adapted people of the Solutrean culture of France and Spain used boats to migrate across the northern Atlantic Ocean to the Americas. In their 2012 book *Across Atlantic Ice*, they theorized that these ancient Europeans had paddled along the edges of the north Atlantic ice more than fifteen thousand years ago. Bruce Bradley argued fairly convincingly that Clovis stone tools were the ancient descendent technology of the Solutreans of Europe. The authors also cited a few early archaeological sites in the eastern United States, including Meadowcroft in Pennsylvania, Cactus Hill in Virginia, and Topper in South Carolina, as evidence that people arrived in the eastern United States before they did in the western United States.

Of course, their hypothesis was met with abundant skepticism, as nearly every American archaeologist accepted the Asian origins of Native Americans as fact. Stanford and Bradley didn't refute that well-established connection. Instead, they suggested that ancient Solutreans traveled to North America only to be overwhelmed genetically and culturally by the later Asian migrants.

One of the most vocal opponents of the Solutrean hypothesis was Lawrence Guy Strauss, a European archaeologist who specialized in the study of Solutrean culture. Strauss argued that Stanford and Bradley's theory had numerous issues. First, Stanford and Bradley argued that the Solutreans followed the Arctic ice sheet, which extended much further south at the time, as they traveled across the edges of the northern Atlantic Ocean. Along the way, these ancient mariners hunted sea mammals that lived near the ice. However, as Strauss argued, there is no evidence that the ancient Solutreans had boats or maritime technology. Instead, they were inland hunter-gatherers of large game animals. In fact, the only data that Stanford and Bradley could find to support a maritime adaptation for Solutrean people were a few images of seals and other sea mammals in ancient rock art found in Spain.

Even more importantly, there is no evidence that Clovis people in the Americas had maritime technology. As with the Solutreans, Clovis people primarily hunted big game found on land. There is not a single Clovis site with evidence—whether it be of technology or food remains—that they had boats, hunted sea mammals, or even fished for that matter. In contrast, archaeologists have effectively shown that Clovis people developed a highly sophisticated stone technology across North America due to their reliance on hunting megafauna such as mammoths, horses, and other now-extinct animals.

Strauss convincingly showed that the similarities in Solutrean and Clovis technology can be explained by their similar subsistence patterns, hunting techniques, and common ancestry. Both the Solutreans of Europe and Clovis of the Americas are descended from central Eurasian peoples. Strauss cited archaeological evidence that Clovis ancestors moved northeasterly from central Asia into Siberia, Alaska, and, eventually, Montana, whereas the ancestors of the ancient Solutreans moved west from Eurasia into Europe. Both Clovis and Solutrean people, then, used similar ancient technology because they evolved from a common human ancestor such as the people that lived nearly thirty thousand years ago at Dolni Vestonice in the Czech Republic. There, ancient Eurasians hunted mammoths and buried their dead with red ochre, much like the Clovis people in Montana eleven thousand years ago.

Nevertheless, despite these alternative explanations for Clovis-Solutrean cultural similarities, Stanford and Bradley continued to push their hypothesis for the European origin of Clovis culture. Despite numerous archaeological attempts, they had not found any solid archaeological links that connected Clovis and Solutrean cultures. For example, they hadn't found any evidence of Clovis people who had carried Solutrean tools or stones with them from Europe. Since their original Solutrean hypothesis in 2004, no additional data has come to light in support of their theory. There are no new archaeological finds since that time that support their hypothesis. The same questions and doubts about their hypothesis remain twenty years later.

Their persistence in pushing forward the Solutrean hypothesis also fueled an anti–Native American sentiment among some people living in the United States. These people believed that Stanford and Bradley's theory showed that Europeans had arrived before Native Americans. Thus, they used this as evidence that the United States government's subjugation and colonization of Indigenous cultures was justified. Since European Americans arrived before Native Americans, some argued, the US government was right in using force to relocate Native American tribes to reservations in the nineteenth and twentieth centuries. Such ideas fueled racism against Native Americans.

The Importance of the Anzick Boy

So, when Eske Willerslev and his colleagues delivered the stunning results of the genetic research on the Anzick boy in Montana, the world paid attention. Was the Anzick boy of European or Asian descent? If the results showed an ancient Solutrean connection, what would that mean for the cultural sovereignty of Native American tribes? How would it affect tribal relations with the US government? If Willerslev's lab showed a European connection to the Anzick boy, it would change everything about human origins in the Americas.

Willerslev and his colleagues showed scientifically that the only Clovis human remains ever found—those of the Anzick boy in Montana—were related to all Native Americans that currently live in both North and South America. More importantly, genetic research established a clear link between the Anzick boy of the eleven-thousand-year-old Clovis culture in Montana and the ancient people that lived in Siberia and northeast Asia more than fifteen thousand years ago. In contrast with the Solutrean hypothesis, Willerslev's research showed no genetic connection to the ancient Solutrean culture of Spain and France at all. The Anzick boy and his Clovis family in Montana descended from people that lived in Asia, not Europe. Therefore, we can say, without question, that the earliest people to live in Montana, as represented by the Anzick boy, traveled there from Asia.

Willerslev and his colleagues' genetic research on the Anzick boy solidified what most archaeologists had already thought regarding the ancient origins of Native Americans. Most of the professional archaeological community had already decided that the Solutrean hypothesis lacked merit due to the lack of supporting archaeological data. However, a handful of stalwarts, including Stanford and Bradley, persisted in their belief, even after the Anzick study. It is amazing that, even in a scientific discipline such as archaeology, unfounded hypotheses persist in the face of all factual evidence. And unfortunately, many Americans continue to cling to what has now become more of a racist ideology than a valid scientific theory. To this day, despite the lack of archaeological data, the Solutrean hypothesis remains popular among some segments of the American public. Unfortunately, Dennis Stanford passed away in 2019 and never recanted his hypothesis, taking it to his grave as his claim to fame.

The magazine *Science* made an obvious mistake in reporting the results of the Anzick genetic study. The "Montana boy" from the Anzick site was only two years old when he passed away, meaning he couldn't possibly have contributed anything to the gene pool of Native Americans after his death. A more accurate title would have been "Native Americans Descend from Family of Montana Boy." The Anzick boy's parents, siblings, and cousins likely lived on beyond his death and spawned hundreds of generations of Native Americans who migrated across North and South America. Their descendants traveled south from Montana into Mexico, Peru, and Argentina. They traveled east into the Mississippi River valley and beyond.

The results of Eske Willerslev and his colleagues' research concluded a long debate about the origins of the earliest people to Montana and the rest of North America. Their genetic study resulted in the most significant finding of any archaeological project in the history of the Big Sky State. But, while the Anzick study was clearly the most important to Montanans, Willerslev has continued to study the genetics of the ancient people of the Americas, well beyond the Anzick boy. Other geneticists have taken up the charge as well, conducting DNA analysis of several additional sets of human remains from Paleoindian archaeological sites in North America.

Eight DNA sites and nine sets of human remains place the earliest Paleoindians into five genetic haplogroups, meaning a group that shares a common ancestor, based on their mitochondrial DNA signatures. The five haplogroups are A, B, C, D, and X, all of which geneticists trace to the ancestral population that lived on the landmass known as Beringia, the area that encompasses Siberia and Alaska today. Starting in Alaska, the remains of two infants from the Upward Sun River (USR) site—who were buried together, yet had different mothers—derived from the B and C haplogroups. The 9,300-year-old Wizard's Beach skeleton in Nevada also belonged to haplogroup C. The 12,400-year-old human coprolites from Paisley Caves in Oregon belonged to two haplogroups, A and B.

Along the Alaska coast, the 10,300-year-old human remains from On-Your-Knees Cave belong to haplogroup D, as do the remains of the two-year-old boy from the Anzick site and the skeleton called Eva from the cave

Archaeologists found these human coprolites in the Paisley Caves site in Oregon. They date to more than twelve thousand years ago, making them among the earliest evidence of people in North America. Brian Lanker photograph, courtesy of Dennis Jenkins

on the Yucatan Peninsula of Mexico. Both of these skeletons date to about 11,000 years ago. Finally, one set of skeletal remains—Kennewick Man in Washington, dated to about 8,400 years ago—is from the minority haplogroup lineage called X. This is the rarest of the haplogroups in modern populations as well as ancient ones, but it still has been shown to derive from the ancestral Beringian hunter-gatherers.

The same genetics found in these nine ancient sets of human remains are represented within the modern Native American populations of North and South America. Indeed, these human remains, including Anzick, represent the founding populations from which all other Indigenous cultures of the Americas derived. The resulting genetic tree connects all Native Americans to their Asian ancestors. Geneticists have already made amazing strides in this effort, and we now know a great deal more about the ancient origins of Native Americans in Montana and elsewhere.

The rest of this chapter examines the DNA results obtained from two archaeological sites—one in Alaska and one in Siberia—to emphasize the genetic relatedness of Montana's Native Americans with their Beringian ancestors. In Russia, the Mal'ta site near Lake Baikal contained the remains of a human child that dated to twenty-four thousand years ago. In central Alaska, as mentioned above, two additional sets of human remains—dating to more than ten thousand years ago—were found at the USR site.

At the Mal'ta site, Russian archaeologists found the remains of a young boy buried under a stone slab along with jewelry made from mammoth ivory. Between 1958 and 1978, the Russian archaeologists continued to excavate the site and found evidence that the people that lived there were megafauna hunters of mammoths, horses, and other large beasts. A figurine found at Mal'ta shows the type of winter clothing used by people who lived at the site around twenty thousand years ago. Similar types of clothing were likely used in winter by the first people to migrate into the Americas and Montana.

Willerslev and his colleagues Maanasa Raghavan and Skoglund Ponus conducted a remarkable genetic study in 2011. *Nature* published their findings three years before Willerslev's Anzick research. As with Anzick, most major newspapers, including the *New York Times*, subsequently reported on the genetic study of the Mal'ta boy in Siberia. Willerslev and his team estimated that "14 to 38 percent of Native American ancestry may originate through gene flow from this ancient population" that lived at the Mal'ta site. Native Americans, then, derived from people who had passed through eastern Siberia, into the Pacific Rim, and onward into the Americas.

In the Anzick study, Willerslev stated that the Anzick boy shared a significant percentage of his genetic composition with this other child who lived

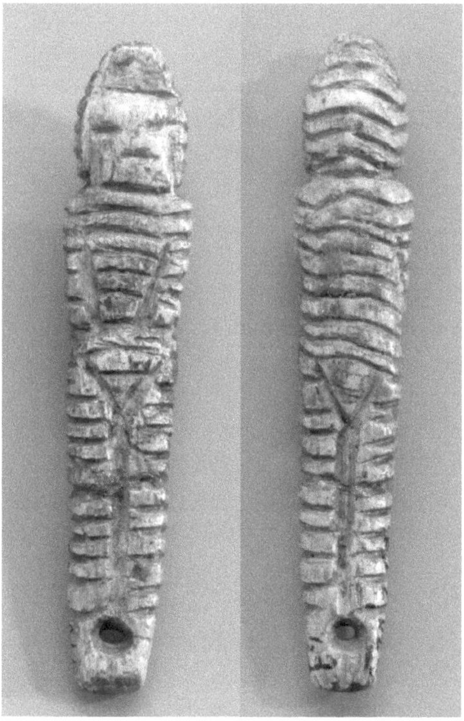

This female figurine (front and back) from the Mal'ta site in Siberia shows the type of clothing worn by people during winter in central Eurasia around twenty thousand years ago.
Courtesy of the State Hermitage Museum, St. Petersburg, Russia

in Siberia twenty-four thousand years ago. The combination of Willerslev's Mal'ta and Anzick studies "shows the same relative affinity to western and eastern Eurasians . . . [suggesting] that the gene flow from the Mal'ta lineage into Native Americans" occurred before the Native American genetic groups that currently live in North and South America split. Today, while all Native Americans are genetically related—due to their common ancestry in Asia—groups living in North and South America are distinct enough that they can be separated into different geographical groups of genetically related people. One important result of Willerslev's research of Anzick and Mal'ta was that this North and South American split occurred after eleven thousand years ago, due to the migration of people related to the Anzick boy across the Americas since that time. So, not only were the boys that lived at Anzick and Mal'ta genetically related, but their ancient families were the people who eventually founded the descendant Native American populations that spread throughout the rest of North and South America.

The Upward Sun River site in Alaska helps us understand the intermediary step that some of these ancient people took on their journey to Montana. The USR site has been the subject of ongoing archaeological excavations by the University of Alaska since the early 2000s. Situated along a small tributary of the Tanana River in central Alaska, it has yielded remarkable evidence of the earliest people to the Americas. Led by archaeologist Ben Potter, the Alaskan team's most amazing discovery was the skeletal remains of two young girls dating to approximately ten thousand years ago. Found during their field season in 2013, the two young girls were buried beneath their house along with stone and bone tools and the remains of salmon, showing that these people were not just hunter-gatherers but also fishers. This makes sense considering that salmon migrate in the thousands through these interior Alaskan rivers and were an abundant food resource for both ancient Native Americans and their recent counterparts.

Potter and his colleagues' genetic study showed that the USR infants descended from the Beringians, the original Native American population to live in the region encompassing Siberia and Alaska. Not only that, but as we stated above, the two infants were from two distinct mitochondrial DNA haplogroups, B and C, indicating that they had different mothers. Obviously, at ten thousand years old, the USR skeletal remains don't represent the first people to arrive in Alaska. As will be discussed in more detail in the next chapter, the earliest archaeological evidence in Alaska indicates that people may have lived there anywhere from two thousand to five thousand years earlier than the people found at the USR site. While some of these first Beringians continued to live in Alaska at places like Upward Sun River, many more of these ancient people moved south, eventually living at places like the Anzick site in Montana.

These three genetic studies—Anzick, Mal'ta, and Upward Sun River—are linked together in telling the origin story of the first Americans. From Siberia, at least twenty-four thousand years ago, the family of the Mal'ta boy moved northeasterly into Beringia. Some of these people established their homes in ancient Beringia and lived there for thousands of years. These early Beringians are represented by the two infant girls buried ten thousand years ago at the USR site in Alaska. Still others of the ancient Beringian population continued through Alaska—sometime between twenty-four thousand and twelve thousand years ago—into the rest of North and South America. By at least eleven thousand years ago, descendants of these ancient Beringian people had moved as far south as Wilsall, Montana, to live at the Anzick site.

While these three ancient sites—as well as the six other genetic sites in North America—help us understand the approximate timeline of human migration, as well as the approximate route of travel, they don't tell us the whole story. Yes, based on the genetic and archaeological finds from the

Led by Ben Potter, researchers from the University of Alaska excavated the Upward Sun River site in Alaska in the early 2010s, where they found two human infants buried together. Radiocarbon dating suggests that these remains—which showed evidence that the children had two different mothers—are more than ten thousand years old.
Courtesy of Ben Potter

sites, we know that ancient people migrated from Asia, through Alaska, and into the Americas at least thirteen thousand or so years ago. But precisely when did this occur? How did they travel? Did they walk from Beringia or use boats? Which route did they take to get to Montana, a coastal route or an interior route? Unfortunately, the three genetic studies from Anzick, Mal'ta, and Upward Sun River can't help us solve the issue of precisely which route was taken to get to Montana from Siberia and Asia, nor can they provide us the precise timeline for the events.

This is where archaeology can contribute to an understanding of the first migrations of people from northeast Asia, Siberia, and Alaska into the Americas. In the next chapters, we'll examine archaeological data of the earliest sites in these areas to help us understand the issue of whether the first migrants to the Americas came down the Pacific Coast or whether they followed an interior route from Alaska.

✷

CHAPTER FOUR

The Lost Continent

Beringia no longer exists, but it once was a vast land covered by tundra, steppe, and forest that encompassed thousands of square miles and connected Russia and the United States. While both nations still have vestiges of the former great continent, today it is bisected by the Bering Strait, with Siberia to the west and Alaska to the east. One of the reasons it is difficult to comprehend the Asian origin of Native Americans is because they had to travel through Beringia, which was long thought to be a snow-and-ice-covered landscape incapable of supporting humans. After decades of scientific research, however, we now know that Beringia was much more like an African savannah than an Arctic wasteland. Beringia contained more than thirty species of now-extinct mammals, including musk oxen, horses, bison, camels, woolly rhinoceros, and mammoths. Since those animals require a huge amount of grass to survive, it makes sense that Beringia was a vast and abundant grassland.

Predators abounded in Beringia as well, including giant bears, sabertooth cats, dire wolves, and humans. Indeed, humans were the major and most-feared predator in this landscape. In pursuit of their prey, people followed the megafauna across the Russian steppe, through Beringia, and into Alaska. Until about fourteen or fifteen thousand years ago, an interior route through Alaska, into Canada, and down to the continental United States was impossible. Two large ice sheets prevented interior travel. The Cordilleran Ice Sheet covered the Pacific Coast, while the Laurentide Ice Sheet covered most of Canada and Alaska.

The two ice sheets created a several-thousand-year bottleneck in eastern Beringia that slowed the progress of migrating animals and people into the Americas. While archaeological evidence of coastal migration is lacking due to rising ocean levels since the Late Pleistocene, some of these early

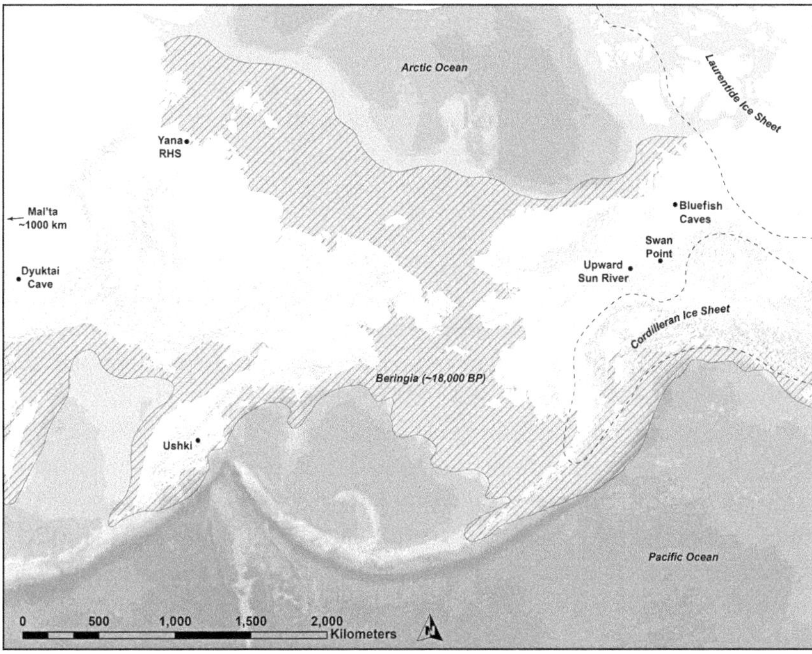

This map shows the boundaries of Beringia in relation to several key archaeological sites in both Russia and Alaska and charts the extent of the Laurentide and Cordilleran Ice Sheets roughly eighteen thousand years ago. Monte White

migrants likely arrived to Beringia by following the shoreline of the Pacific Ocean. They may have moved by kayak and umiak along the Pacific Coast hunting seals, whales, and fish.

Archaeological data is abundant, however, for the ancient hunter-gatherers of the interior areas of Beringia. Interior hunter-gatherers lived along the major rivers of Beringia and hunted mammoths, rhinoceros, sloths, camels, and horses. The genetic data indicate that these migrating human populations lived in the wilds of Beringia for a few thousand years or more before proceeding southward into the Americas. For generations, these people saw nothing but ice when they looked east and south. A few intrepid explorers pushed across the ice, returning with stories of more ice. They likely advised staying in Beringia rather than risking their lives on the barren ice sheets. As established in the earlier chapter on genetics, these ancient Beringians—hunter-gatherers who lived off the sea and the land—are the ancestors of today's Indigenous tribes of North and South America, including Montana.

Hunter-Gatherers: Some Basics

Risk minimization is a hallmark trait of hunter-gatherers worldwide. One of my earliest anthropology professors as an undergraduate student was Richard Gould. In the late 1960s and early 1970s, Gould lived with hunter-gatherers in Australia. As reviewed in his 1980 book *Living Archaeology*, his goal was to study their ways of life to better understand archaeological sites. This method of study—ethnoarchaeology—seeks to learn the truths of the past by studying modern people. While living among Aboriginal people in Australia, Gould learned that they often made important decisions about where to travel and what to eat using the simple principle of risk minimization. Given the small sizes of their family groups—between ten and thirty people within each band—they really couldn't afford to endanger themselves, so they made decisions that reduced their chance of death or mortal injury rather than ones that might prove more lucrative, as is common in many modern societies. For example, if given the choice between sticking with the effective hunting technology that they had used for hundreds and thousands of years or adopting a new technology that might work better, they would stick with their existing technology. It worked for thousands of years, so why rock the boat? Risk minimization is the main reason that most hunter-gatherers take a very conservative approach to technological innovation. If you minimize your risk of failure, you maximize your chances of survival.

It seems that hunter-gatherers of Beringia likely chose to reduce their risk and increase their chances of long-term survival by staying in Beringia rather than traversing the icy landscapes that encompassed the two vast ice sheets. The opportunities to find adequate food, wood, and shelter on the ice were scant compared to staying on the vast and productive Beringian continent.

There would have been two likely opportunities for land mammals, plants, and humans to migrate south during the Late Pleistocene. One was during an interstadial—or warming period—approximately twenty-eight thousand years ago. During this period of warming during the Late Pleistocene, human hunter-gatherers expanded their ranges to the north. Based on the archaeological sites in Russia, such as the Yana Rhinoceros Horn site (Yana RHS), humans colonized northeastern Russia during this warming period. While there is no archaeological evidence in Beringia to support this notion, it was possible for human hunter-gatherers to have moved through Beringia into the Americas at that time. For example, if the footprints of humans at White Sands National Park, New Mexico, are actually more than twenty thousand years old, the twenty eight thousand-year interstadial would have reduced glacial advances enough to allow humans to migrate along the coast.

Starting twenty-five thousand years ago, however, this planet experienced what is referred to as the Last Glacial Maximum (LGM) of the Late Pleistocene epoch. This was a period of intensive cooling and glacial expansion that persisted for another seven thousand years. It was during this period—between twenty-five and eighteen thousand years ago—that hunter-gatherers populated Beringia and expanded their hunting, gathering, and fishing ranges to the east and north, from northeastern Russia and Eurasia into Alaska and the Beringian continent, both along the Pacific Coast as well as through the interior.

The hunter-gatherers of Beringia likely migrated not only within their principal areas—coast and interior—but also between the two areas. For example, today, hunter-gatherers in Alaska live on the coast for some period of the year but go to the interior to hunt caribou during other times of the year. They are seasonally transhumant, meaning they move between the coast and the interior as necessary to make a living. In Beringia, following the principle of transhumance, both the interior and coastal groups were in contact with each other, perhaps socializing, trading, and intermarrying.

Between twenty-five thousand and fifteen thousand years ago, give or take a thousand years, it appears that coastal and interior peoples lived in Beringia together, becoming the original ancestral people of all Native American cultures living today. DNA studies have shown that the Beringia bottleneck was the melting pot from which all subsequent Native American tribes originated. Those people carry genes of interior Siberian peoples as well as those of coastal Asian peoples.

If people did not reach Beringia prior to twenty-eight thousand years ago—and there is scant evidence that they did—it is possible that a few of the earliest people to Beringia, likely the coastal group, might have decided to push their way along the ice-blocked coast. If they had used boats and moved along the edge of what is today the Aleutian Islands of Alaska, they might have found enough sea life to support their eastward and southward migrations, with the ultimate hope of finding more land as they moved south. Perhaps it is this persistent group—ignoring the risk minimization principle—that eventually were the first to see the ice-free coastlines of present-day British Columbia, Washington, Oregon, and California. These early coastal migrants likely also potentially made their way into the interior, perhaps hunting giant sloths and leaving their footprints in New Mexico twenty thousand years ago or so.

While a small group of ocean travelers may have pushed their way along the coast, it is apparent from recent scientific research that the vast majority of the early migrants to Beringia likely stayed on that continent for many

This early twentieth-century photograph shows a group of Apsáalooke men in traditional dress. The Apsáalooke people are among the many Indigenous nations in North America descended from the Beringians.
Lot 035 B11F09.04, Montana Historical Society Photograph Archives

generations. The DNA evidence shows clearly that Beringia's population is ancestral to the subsequent Native American populations of the Americas. The Apsáalooke (Crow) tribe of Montana, the Apaches of Arizona, the Crees of Minnesota, the Five Nations (Iroquois) of New York, and the Seminoles of Florida all descended from this Beringian melting pot, the ancestral home of all American Indigenous peoples.

While a small portion of that population eventually migrated down the coast, most people stayed in Beringia. Why would they leave? There were vast resources for hunter-gatherers and an abundance of sea life and land life that provided a bounty of resources. It is also likely that coastal people traveled the interior to hunt land mammals, while interior people likely traveled to the coast to fish and hunt sea mammals. In this way, the two groups—interior and coastal—blended together into one people that carried genetic material from both Asia and interior Siberia to become Beringians.

What Was Beringia Like?

Both the interior and coastal areas of Beringia were rich in resources and provided outstanding opportunities for human colonization during the LGM. Interior-adapted people lived in river and creek valleys, hunting the megafauna and collecting plants among the hills and steppes of the region. In present-day Russia, western Beringia contained river basins such as the Lena, Indigirka, and Kolyma that flowed into the Arctic Ocean. In eastern Beringia, in what is today Alaska and the Yukon, three large mountain ranges are divided into large, flat river basins, including the Pacific Coast Range, the Alaska Range, and the Brooks Range.

The climate of Beringia during the LGM was much colder and drier than today. Summer temperatures measured more than fifteen degrees Fahrenheit cooler during summer, while winter temperatures were likely similar. The drier climate, however, meant that Beringia remained free of snow and ice for most of the year. Glaciers expanded due to the reduced summer temperatures, eventually growing big enough to block migration by animals, plants, and humans to the east and south. Research into the LGM shows that it likely reached its icy peak between twenty-seven thousand and eighteen thousand years ago, with ice covering the Bering Sea for all but a few months per year. This time range varies across Beringia, with some areas in Alaska remaining covered in ice until thirteen thousand years ago. It wasn't until the LGM began to wane—approximately eighteen thousand years ago or so—that glaciers began to melt and more-modern landscapes started to appear.

While a small group or groups of intrepid Beringians may have pushed south through this icy landscape during a summer warm spell, most ancestral Native Americans likely stayed in the continent until after the LGM was over and temperatures warmed, sometime around eighteen thousand to fifteen thousand years ago. During this period of the Late Pleistocene, the coastal glaciers would have sufficiently melted for humans to move down the coast. A little bit later, perhaps thirteen thousand to fourteen thousand years ago, an interior route between the two glacial masses—the Cordilleran and the Laurentide—opened up as well, allowing people, animals, and plants to colonize interior Alaska, Canada, and eventually Montana.

Beringia itself only existed because of the massive glaciers of the Late Pleistocene, which stretched across North America, from the Pacific to the Atlantic Ocean, and as far south as Montana. While Beringia was spared from ice for the most part, ice likely covered most of Canada during the Late Pleistocene. The massive glaciers also required lots of water, essentially sucking up billions of cubic feet of water from the world's oceans. Because of the ice sheets, the world's oceans were shallower than they are today, with coastlines and beaches much further away from the shoreline than they are today. Recent science on the topic has shown that global sea levels dropped more than 320 feet during the Late Pleistocene and exposed the continental shelf along the Pacific Ocean shoreline, including the area that now separates Siberia and Alaska—the Bering Strait.

Scott Elias of the University of London has created a map of the Late Pleistocene shoreline that visualizes the Beringian continent. He estimates that Russia and Alaska were connected by a land bridge that was essentially the size of the state of Texas, measuring more than six hundred miles wide, and existed between approximately thirty thousand and at least fifteen thousand radiocarbon years ago. During the LGM, more than 40 percent of the entire state of Alaska lay beneath massive ice sheets. However, that also means that 60 percent of the state was open to humans, animals, and plants. Eighteen thousand years ago or so, warming temperatures started to melt the glaciers, eventually to the point that the Bering Strait separated Beringia into its western and eastern areas, likely sometime after thirteen thousand years ago.

The shallower oceans of the Late Pleistocene present a huge problem for archaeological research of Beringia and all coastally adapted peoples of that time. These people may have lived on beaches and adjacent terraces along the Pacific coastline, and today those landscapes are covered by tens and hundreds of feet of ocean. The modern shorelines along the Pacific Coast were not, for the most part, the same as those used by their ancient counterparts during the Late Pleistocene. Beringia itself would not have existed if not for the lower ocean levels. While the Bering Strait separates Russia and Alaska today, the lower ocean levels of the Late Pleistocene allowed the two continents to be connected. During the waning years of the Last Glacial Maximum, ocean water levels gradually rose as glaciers melted, submerging much of the Beringian landscape and eventually forming the Bering Strait between Alaska and Siberia. At the same time, the rising ocean levels at the end of the Late Pleistocene submerged the ancient settlements along the former shorelines, meaning most archaeological sites with evidence of these early migrations along the coast have disappeared beneath the rising seas.

While the archaeological data for coastal hunter-gatherers is scant for sites dating to the Late Pleistocene, there is every reason to hypothesize that such populations existed. Ancient Beringians likely lived and traveled along the coast, but a coast that is no longer present in most places. So, for now, much of our interpretation of their ancient lifestyle remains speculation. Future research in underwater archaeology and other innovative archaeological survey strategies are turning up more and more ancient sites that will hopefully fill in our knowledge regarding these early Pacific Coast hunter-gatherers.

Much of what we know about ancient Beringians is based on studies of modern Indigenous people who live as hunter-gatherers along the Pacific Rim. The coastal hunter-gatherers in Beringia likely lived a way of life not dissimilar to that of their ancestors in Japan or their descendants in Oregon and Washington. They lived above beaches on high terrace landforms, keeping their canoes and umiaks on the beaches in front of their houses. Beaches were likely areas of intensive activity, with men, women, and children conducting daily survival tasks such as maintaining fishing nets, making stone tools, or carving whale ivory into spear shafts. They likely constructed their houses using wood, bone, grasses, and leather. It is not clear from the archaeological research if their houses were above-ground or partially subterranean. Pithouses were common among hunter-gatherer cultures of Alaska and Canada in more recent history, so they may have been used as far back as the Late Pleistocene in Beringia as well.

Archaeological Evidence of Beringian Settlement

Is there any way for archaeologists to find settlements of the earliest Beringians in Alaska and Russia? Modern archaeologists are currently studying two different types of landscapes to try to find some of those ancient Beringian settlements. First, they are studying underwater and offshore settings using modern submersible technologies. This type of archaeological survey is incredibly difficult due to tens of feet of ocean silts that have covered ancient sites, as well as simply the vagaries of looking for archaeological sites in the rough waters of the north Pacific Ocean.

Because of the difficulties of finding ancient sites under the ocean, many archaeologists have turned to land-based surveys. These archaeologists work in areas along the modern shoreline that were once amenable to human occupation during the Late Pleistocene, seeking high landforms in California, Washington, Oregon, Alaska, and Russia that were above water during the LGM. Since these high landforms along the coast and in the interior may have remained above water and/or glacier-free, they potentially contain evidence of early Beringian settlements.

So, based on this type of research—both inland and offshore—what evidence is there that people lived in Beringia during the Last Glacial Maximum? The Beringian Standstill Hypothesis, which posits that the ancestors of modern Native Americans hit a population bottleneck during the LGM, argues that the population was stuck there and unable to migrate. While

DNA data tells us that this population standstill indeed took place, it has been difficult for both water-based and land-based archaeologists to find these early sites. Most of the coastal areas of human settlement are underwater. Land-based archaeologists, meanwhile, face the challenge of conducting archaeological surveys in mostly uninhabited, remote regions of Alaska and Russia.

Land-based archaeologists are tasked with attempting to survey 250 million acres of land in Alaska for archaeological sites. Beringian human populations were likely very low, with a total of perhaps only ten thousand. Consider that Alaska today contains less than 1 million people, most of them clustered in a few larger cities such as Anchorage and Fairbanks. Most of the state remains unpopulated, but it still maintains a population density that is more than fifty to one hundred times more than the Beringian hunter-gatherer population during the LGM.

Consider also that hunter-gatherers are highly mobile, often not spending more than a day or so in any given location. This means that finding a hunter-gatherer archaeological site is sort of like finding a needle in a haystack. As they moved across the landscape searching for food, Beringian hunter-gatherers left behind ephemeral evidence of their existence. Over fifteen thousand years, these traces often just disappeared under vegetation or into rivers, overtaken by forests and floods. In addition to the age and deterioration of the ephemeral hunter-gatherer camp sites, imagine that the haystack encompasses more than 2 million acres. Now imagine trying to find a needle that is over fifteen thousand years old and covered by up to one hundred inches of forest duff and dirt.

Given that only a handful of dedicated archaeologists are on the job in Alaska (and even fewer in Russia), overall progress in trying to discover ancient Beringian archaeological sites has been slow going. Only a small handful of sites dating to the LGM have been found in Alaska and Russia. In a 2017 academic article in the journal *Current Anthropology*, Kelly Graf of Texas A&M University and Ian Buvit of Central Washington University have provided an excellent summary of these Beringian sites, both on the Russian and American sides of the Bering Strait. The authors accept the Beringian Standstill Hypothesis, which stands as the most viable explanation of Beringian and American migrations. They propose two pulses of human movement through the region: first, the movement of coastal and inland human populations into Beringia some twenty thousand years ago or so; and second, the movement of the Beringian source population south into the Americas after fifteen thousand years ago. I've suggested that there might have been an even earlier pulse, or movement, of people southward perhaps resulting in the early footprints in New Mexico. So far, there is only one site—the White Sands site—to support that earlier, ephemeral human movement. There are, however, "new" old sites discovered every year, some of which may help support the hypothesis that there may have been an early pulse of human movement into the Americas.

For now, what do Graf and Buvit say are the key sites in Beringia? In Siberia (northeastern Russia), the earliest archaeological sites show human occupation as early as forty-seven thousand years ago, with most dating to after thirty thousand years ago. These sites support the hypothesis that humans lived in the far northeastern reaches of Russia, the western edges of Beringia at that time. This certainly bolsters the Beringian Standstill Hypothesis in the sense that there was in fact a human population in Siberia that eventually moved east into Beringia.

The most important Siberian site from this period is Mal'ta. As discussed earlier in this book, DNA analysis of the Mal'ta skeleton indicates that this person shared ancestry with Native Americans. This implies that at least some portion of that Eurasian population migrated to Beringia. These early Siberian populations lived in river valleys within the interior of Russia and hunted now-extinct megafauna, including mammoths and rhinoceros. Stone tools from Siberian archaeological sites indicate that people used European-style Upper Paleolithic blade technology. Long, linear flakes were produced from stone cores that were then used to tip projectile points for hunting. Personal adornments were found at some sites, including bone and stone beads and pendants as jewelry. Some of the settlements may have been semi-permanent base camps from which hunter-gatherers traveled daily to hunt, gather, and fish for food. The substantial house structures, built to withstand the harshest of winters, likely used bone and wood for a circular structure, with the roof and walls covered with animal hides.

After thirty thousand years ago, site counts in western Beringia (Russia) increase in frequency, as typified by the Yana RHS. This site marks the first human movements toward the edges of the Arctic Circle at a latitude of 71 degrees north. Once humans reached that region, they started to push east toward Beringia, likely limited to the north by the icy seas of the Arctic.

Animals identified at sites like Yana RHS and others in western Beringia include woolly mammoth, rhinoceros, horse, bison, elk, sheep, mountain goat, antelope, deer, fox, and hare. The habitat appears similar to that of Beringia, a fact that likely helped when people began the push toward Alaska thirty thousand years ago.

The Russian sites also have an Upper Paleolithic flair. The anthropomorphic figurines found at sites like Mal'ta even show the winter clothing worn by people of the time. These figurines resemble those produced by the human populations to the south and west of Russia, suggesting a cultural affiliation or connection to inland Europe. Other examples of art include engraved ivory plaques and rods and figurines made to resemble mammoths and birds. Numerous bone projectile points were found at the site, as well as a bone engraved with a mammoth, one of the earliest examples of art in Siberia.

Archaeologists consider the Dyuktai Cave site in Siberia to be one of the hallmark Russian Late Pleistocene sites. In fact, the culture from this period is often referred to as Dyuktai Culture. Dated to about seventeen thousand years ago, the site yielded an Upper Paleolithic toolkit comprised of several microblades, bifaces, and other stone tools used in the hunting of large game. Bifaces, stone tools produced by shearing off two sides of a stone, helped sharpen projectile points and knives, and are considered a standard technology used by early Native American populations. In his 2016 article on Siberian archaeology, Yan Axel Gómez Coutouly of France's Institute for Archaeology and Ethnology states that the Dyuktai Culture produced microblades from wedge-shaped cores. The microblades were inset into antler/bone/ivory projectile points. In addition to microblades, several large bifaces were found at Dyuktai Cave, suggesting a possible ancestral connection to North American toolkits from the Clovis era, which are dominated by bifacial lithic technology. The Dyuktai toolkit also resembles the ones used at several Alaskan sites. Some archaeologists have referred to this toolkit as the Paleoarctic Tradition, encompassing Siberian and Alaskan sites within the region of Beringia.

After twenty-five thousand years ago or so, archaeologists have had difficulty locating many sites that indicate eastward movements into Beringia. Ushki, an important site in Kamchatka, represents a near-coastal human settlement along a river valley. The Ushki site is in an interior setting, but it appears that the site—dating to about thirteen thousand years ago—contains evidence of fishing. Given its proximity to the Pacific Coast, it certainly provides tantalizing evidence that a coastal population lived in the region during the LGM.

The research of Ted Goebel of Texas A&M University and several American and Russian colleagues at Ushki shows that the coastal populations of the Pacific pushed north along the Pacific Rim. Interestingly, people at the site utilized stemmed projectile points to haft their hunting implements. This type of projectile is more common at sites along the Pacific Coast of North America as well as within the Great Basin region. Does the presence of stemmed projectile points at Ushki indicate a cultural connection with people that migrated to the Americas?

The Ushki site is located near the launching point from which people might have used kayaks or umiaks to migrate eastward along the Aleutian Islands of Alaska and ultimately to the Pacific Coast of North America. So, while this site is not as old as archaeologists would like to see, it points to a maritime adaptation that involved similar bifacial technology as found in the Americas during the LGM and the presence of a human population living along or very near the coast. This is rare. Very few sites have been found along the Pacific Rim of Beringia that support the idea of a coastal migration. The Ushki site, as a result, is a very important site, one that helps support the coastal migration hypothesis for the founding of early America.

Another important site in the region is Swan Point in Alaska, which dates to around twelve thousand years ago and contains stone tool technology similar to that found further west in Russia, namely in the use of blades to tip projectile points and the use of retouched scrapers and burins—chisel-like objects—in daily life. These sorts of tools were used by hunter-gatherers to make clothing and process hides in Late Pleistocene Alaska. As with the Ushki site in Kamchatka, archaeologists see the introduction of bifacial technology into the toolkits in eastern Beringia (Alaska) at Swan Point. The introduction of such technologies twelve thousand to thirteen thousand

The Bluefish Caves site in the Yukon yielded potential evidence of early people in eastern Beringia. Jacques Cinq-Mars, seen here, excavated the site in the late 1970s, but it has since been the subject of controversy over its antiquity. Courtesy of Ruth Gotthardt

years ago at Swan Point and Ushki was an important innovation that appears to have pushed south into the Americas with early migrants.

Bluefish Caves in the Yukon, near Alaska's eastern border, is one of the more famous archaeological sites that contains tantalizing evidence of early people in eastern Beringia. Excavations at the site have yielded some of the oldest evidence of humans and animals in Beringia. Radiocarbon dating suggests that a cut-marked jawbone, indicating that humans butchered a horse at the site, is twenty-four thousand years old. The linear cut marks on the jaw resemble the ones that hunter-gatherers created when they removed the animal's tongue. Many archaeologists, however, have doubts about the presence of humans at the site, and instead suggest that the "cut marks" on the jaw stem from carnivore teeth scraping on the bone.

Authors of an article in the scientific journal *PLOS One* suggest that this archaeological site confirms the accuracy of the Beringian Standstill Hypothesis, showing that people were present as far east in Alaska as they could reach during the LGM. Other archaeologists, such as Graf and Buvit, remain skeptical of the site because the evidence of humans there appears ambiguous. Are the cut marks on the bone really the result of human activity, or is it possible that the lines were produced by natural weathering or even gnawing on the bones by animals? The lack of a definite association between stone tools at the site and the twenty-four-thousand-year-old bone means that some in the archaeological community regard the site with skepticism.

However, Lauriane Bourgeon, the lead author of the *PLOS One* article, states that the site has a typical Upper Paleolithic toolkit, including microblades similar to those found in sites further west in Russia such as Dyuktai Cave. Still, the evidence is not definitive because microblades continued to be used in Alaska well into the Holocene, the geological era that began around ten thousand years ago. While the exact age of the microblades remains uncertain, the evidence so far indicates that archeologists need to continue exploring Bluefish Caves and other sites in the area for additional evidence of humans in eastern Beringia.

As discussed in a previous chapter, Upward Sun River (USR), one of the most important sites in Alaska, has yielded DNA data from human skeletal remains that indicate a long-term occupation of the interior of Alaska during the LGM. This tantalizing data seemingly proves that there was a human population in Beringia that served as the predecessor to every Native American group in North America. Remember, however, that the USR site only dates to about ten thousand years ago. So, while it is important for the understanding of the Beringian Standstill Hypothesis and the relationship between Native Americans and Beringians, the USR site isn't

Archaeologists at Bluefish Caves found parallel incisions on this jawbone, perhaps indicating that humans butchered a horse at the site around twenty-four thousand years ago. Courtesy of Ruth Gotthardt

really that old, certainly not as old as we need it to be to absolutely prove the standstill hypothesis to be true.

Graf and Buvit acknowledge a deficiency of Beringian sites that date to sometime between the thirty-thousand-year-old Yana RHS in Russia and the fourteen-thousand-year-old Swan Point site in Alaska. What happened in between? Does the dearth of abundant archaeological evidence mean that the Beringian Standstill Hypothesis is bunk? Why doesn't the archaeology necessarily support the DNA data? As we have already discussed, it is extremely difficult to find archaeological sites in such a vast landscape, and the minimal amount of actual surveying done in these areas hasn't been productive so far. As with surveying the underwater settings, we may see that future research enhances our understanding of Beringian archaeology. At this point, there are simply not enough sites dating to the period between thirty thousand and fifteen thousand years ago to support the Beringian Standstill Hypothesis as set forth by the DNA data. Nevertheless, sites like Bluefish Caves, Swan Point, and Upward Sun River in Alaska, as well as the Yana RHS, Dyuktai Cave, and Ushki sites in Siberia and Kamchatka, provide enough evidence that archaeologists should continue to look for sites in Beringia. There is a great deal to learn about the culture of the people that lived there and who eventually became the source population for millions of Native Americans, including those that traveled to Montana more than eleven thousand years ago.

*

CHAPTER FIVE

Pacific Coast Connections

So far, this book has proposed that the ancestors of the first humans to settle in Montana moved from Eurasia on a north-northeasterly trajectory through Siberia and western Beringia before experiencing a population standstill about fifteen thousand years ago or so in Alaska. Based largely on the DNA similarities between ancient Beringians and Native Americans, the Beringian Standstill Hypothesis suggests that humans likely stopped migrating through Beringia when they encountered the conjoined Cordilleran and Laurentide Ice Sheets, which blocked their way east and south into the Americas. Despite the lack of archaeological site data in Beringia, the available evidence indicates that humans lived in Beringia from twenty-five thousand to fifteen thousand years ago.

We've also posited that people could have subsequently migrated into the Americas using an inland route or a coastal route. People likely used both routes at the end of the Last Glacial Maximum (LGM), sometime after fifteen thousand years ago. The next two chapters will consider whether the original Native American population of Montana originated from a coastal migration that turned inward or from an exclusively interior migration down the Ice-Free Corridor. In addition, they aim to determine if Indigenous people were in the Americas before 11,500 years ago. Recall that one of the major debates in American archaeology is whether any people in the Americas predated the Clovis culture. For many years, Clovis was thought to be the original American culture. However, today, most archaeologists agree—often with much debate—that people were in the Americas before Clovis. These early sites are often referred to as pre-Clovis. Archaeologists have yet to agree as to how those ancient Americans arrived. This chapter focuses on the coastal migration hypothesis, which is gaining traction among American archaeologists for a variety of reasons.

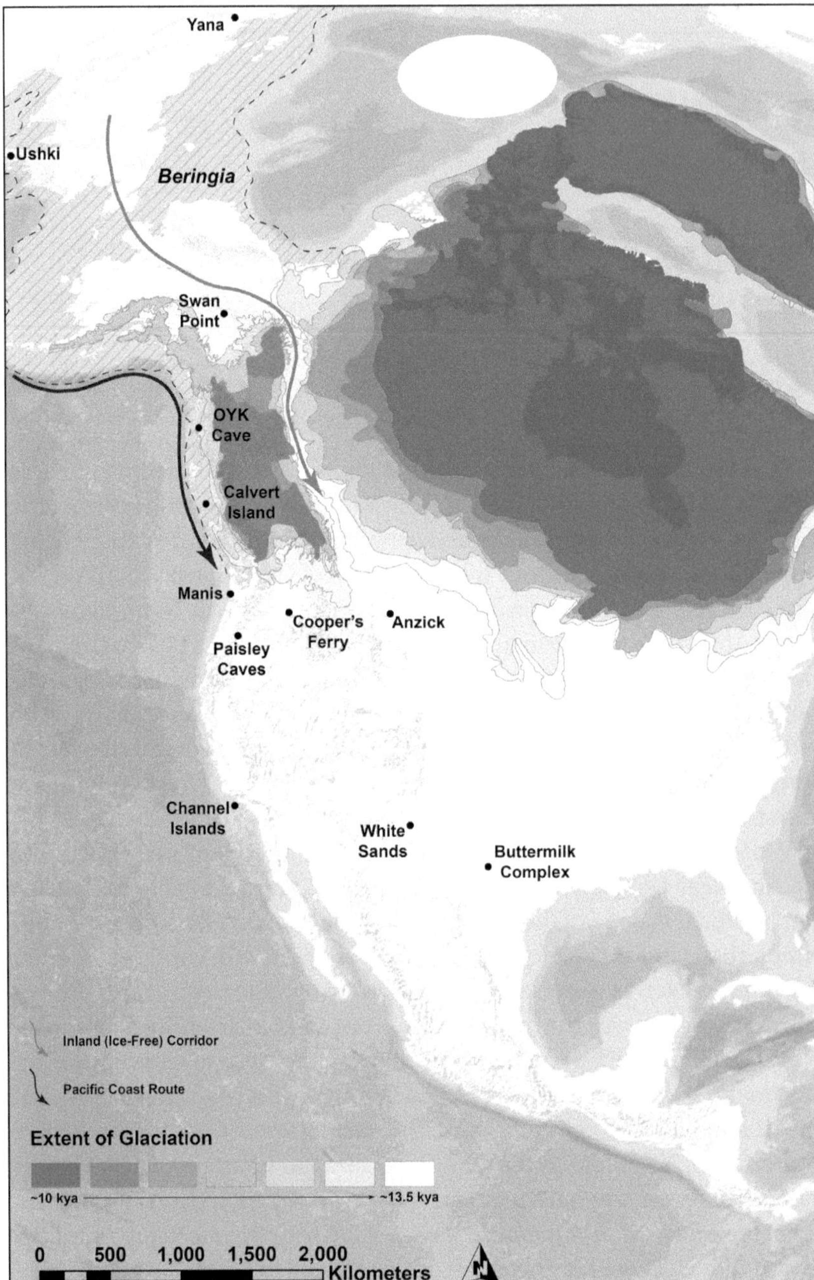

This map indicates the earliest archaeological sites in North America relative to the extent of glaciation during the Last Glacial Maximum. Monte White

While most archaeologists thought that the Clovis culture had descended from people who had migrated through the Ice-Free Corridor, Knut Fladmark saw it differently. In the 1970s, he became one of the earliest American archaeologists to suggest that people may have migrated to the Americas along the coast. Among the archaeologists pushing the Pacific Coast hypothesis today is Jon Erlandson from the University of Oregon. He has suggested that first peoples migrated down the coast following a "Kelp Highway." He claims that the northern Pacific Coast—both thirteen thousand years ago as well as today—supports a unique marine habitat consisting of kelp (seaweed) forests that provide ample resources to support abundant maritime life, including large sea mammals and fish. Erlandson proposes that early Native Americans migrated down the Pacific Coast long before Clovis by finding subsistence in the kelp forests that existed across the north Pacific, from Japan to Beringia to California.

The Pacific Coast theory includes two possible migration scenarios: first, the Early Coastal Migration (ECM) model, which may have occurred before twenty thousand years ago; and second, the Coastal Migration (CM) model, which likely occurred after fifteen thousand years ago. The CM model is supported by archaeological evidence, while the ECM model is merely hypothetical and lacks significant archaeological support, except for the footprints at White Sands, New Mexico. Despite this lack of evidence, the ECM model deserves our consideration, if only to help us determine the conditions that may have allowed this migration to occur during or just before the end of the LGM.

The Early Coastal Migration Model

The discovery of twenty-three-thousand-year-old human footprints at White Sands National Park in New Mexico has forced archaeologists to consider the plausibility of a very early migration of early Native Americans along the Pacific Coast of North America. As far as we know, the interior route was closed at this time, blocking a land-based population in Alaska from pushing south. So, if people arrived in New Mexico more than twenty thousand years ago, they must have traveled along the coast.

The Early Coastal Migration model posits that while much of the human population remained in Beringia, blocked by the ice sheets, a small contingent continued east and south along the coastline into the Americas. The archaeological data clearly indicate that humans lived in Beringia twenty-five thousand years ago. The Yana Rhinoceros Horn site in western Beringia (Russia), among a handful of others reviewed in the previous chapter, indicates that a significant and well-adapted hunter-gatherer population resided in the region. The Bluefish Caves site in Alaska also contains controversial archaeological data in support of the idea that humans reached far western Beringia twenty-three thousand years ago. From this evidence, it appears likely that much of Beringia was populated, albeit sparsely.

There is far less archaeological data to support the second part of the ECM model: the migration itself. If, as some archaeologists contend, the White Sands footprints are only twelve thousand to thirteen thousand years old instead of twenty thousand to twenty-three thousand years old, then there is almost no archaeological data to support the ECM. If the migration indeed occurred at that time, it might have been a fairly quick expedition by a small human population. The climate and environmental data show that some portions of the coastal route would have contained less ice around twenty-five thousand years ago than at any time during the subsequent ten thousand years.

So, ancestral Native Americans could have pushed south prior to twenty-five thousand years ago along the Pacific Coast, perhaps cutting themselves off from the Beringian standstill population for several thousand years.

During his travels in Alaska, Edward S. Curtis photographed these Indigenous fishermen in kayaks in 1929. Native peoples living in present-day Alaska and the Canadian coast have long made use of kayaks and umiaks for sea travel, and Beringians traversing the Pacific Coast likely used similar vessels over 11,500 years ago. Library of Congress

Given that they had moved slowly but surely all the way up the Pacific Rim—following the kelp highway—from Asia into Alaska, why wouldn't they have simply kept going? While that is a good question, it largely remains unanswered.

It is possible that a small population, or a series of small population pulses, traveled south along the coast during the LGM, sometime after twenty-five thousand years ago. While risky, it could have been a daring move to explore along the edges of the ice sheets that blocked passage along the coast in the Aleutian Islands of Alaska. This might have been possible if the travelers were in kayaks and umiaks, since they would have been able to hunt sea mammals and fish for subsistence along the edges of the ice flows. Presumably, these intrepid hunters and fishers would have pulled their boats onto the sea ice to make camp at night during their explorations along the coast. There is, however, absolutely no archaeological data to support either scenario. The remainder of this chapter focuses on the Coastal Migration model, which posits an early Pacific Coast route used by Native Americans from Beringia after fifteen thousand years ago.

Late Pleistocene Maritime Adaptations in the Pacific Rim of Asia

Before delving into the archaeological data in support of the Coastal Migration model in the Americas, let's set the stage. The last chapter reviewed the data that clearly show that people arrived in the northern reaches of Beringia by at least twenty-five thousand to thirty thousand years ago. These Beringians killed woolly mammoths, rhinoceros, and bison, among other megafauna, in order to live on the grassy steppes. All of the sites in Beringia—at least the ones discovered so far—show an interior hunter-gatherer adaptation, not a coastal one. Even the Ushki site in Kamchatka is an interior site, although it is within thirty miles of the Pacific Coast and indicates a subsistence pattern reliant at least in part on fishing. What other data exist to support a coastal adaptation of hunter-gatherers in the Pacific Rim during the Late Pleistocene?

Australia

The human discovery of the Australian continent is not directly relevant to our discussion of the first people of Montana, but it merits consideration here. Certainly, no direct relationship between early Australians and early Americans exists. There is no archaeological data to suggest that Australians paddled their way across the Pacific to the Americas twenty thousand years ago. In fact, there is abundant archaeological evidence that the islands of the Pacific—including Hawaii, Easter Island, Samoa, among others—

were the last places on earth to be settled by people, less than three thousand years ago, more than fifteen thousand years after humans from Asia populated the Americas. Australia, then, matters not due to any direct connection to Montana, but because it provides evidence of a Pacific Rim maritime adaptation by humans during the Late Pleistocene.

Humans reached the Pacific Rim of Asia more than seventy thousand years ago. A recent article in the journal *Nature* by Chris Clarkson and colleagues indicates that people arrived in Australia as early as sixty-five thousand years ago. Archaeological evidence even shows that people had also reached places like far southeastern Asia by that time. Just as Beringia was the launching point for humans into the Americas, the island archipelagos of southeast Asia were the starting point for the migration of people to the Australian continent. Australia, however, has always—even during the low-ocean levels of the Late Pleistocene—been disconnected from the land mass of Asia. While some of the islands of New Guinea were connected to Australia, forming a larger supercontinent called Sahul, the sixty-mile-wide Timor Strait still separated this landmass from mainland Asia.

The discovery of archaeological sites dating to at least fifty thousand years ago in the Northern Territories of Australia begs for an explanation. If the geologists told us that oceans separated southeast Asia from Australia at that time, how did people get there? Well, they must have used boats to travel the fifty to sixty miles across the Timor Strait from Asia to Australia. Coastal Australian Aboriginal populations, as well as those that live in the islands of New Guinea, still use maritime technology to live along their coastlines. Those traveling up to sixty thousand years ago likely used boats manufactured from bamboo, perhaps fitted with outriggers, to navigate the choppy ocean waters off the Australian coastline, as well as nets and spears to fish for their subsistence. This means of adaptation allowed early Aborigines to arrive in their eventual homelands in continental Australia.

The obvious implication of the peopling of Australia is that humans in southeast Asia had maritime technology more than fifty thousand years ago. While we don't know exactly what those boats looked like—since none have ever been found by archaeologists—we know without a doubt that people used them in their earliest travels from Asia to Australia. Remember that the DNA data discussed in chapter 3 indicate the presence of some East Asian DNA in the admixture that ultimately blended in Beringia to form the ancestral population of Native Americans. So, if people living in East Asia had boats, it seems more than likely that some portion of those people used a maritime adaptation to move north along the Pacific Rim of Asia to reach Beringia earlier than twenty thousand years ago.

The Founding of Japan

The ever-expanding human settlement of the world reached the Pacific Ocean more than fifty thousand years ago, with some of the people continuing by boat to Australia. Still others continued up the Pacific Coast toward Japan. Archaeological data support a coastal adaptation for early hunter-gatherer-fishers in present-day Japan. Humans settled the main islands of Honshu and Hokkaido as early as thirty-five thousand to forty thousand years ago, perhaps even earlier. Archaeologists have found cultural connections, including similar artifacts and stone tool types, between Japanese hunter-gatherer-fishers and those living in Kamchatka and Taiwan. This indicates that coastal movement took place between the northern reaches of Hokkaido and Kamchatka and between mainland Japan and Taiwan during the Late Pleistocene. The trips between Japan, Kamchatka, and Taiwan required the use of boats in open ocean settings. We also know that people living in Japan more than thirty-five thousand years ago used boats to reach offshore islands. The best evidence for this is the fact that mainland Japanese archaeological sites have yielded obsidian collected from Kozushima Island, located more than thirty miles offshore. People used boats to travel from mainland Japan to the island to collect rock for stone tool production at least twenty thousand years ago, if not more.

Late Pleistocene cultures in Japan relied on a wide variety of stone tools but primarily employed microblade technology similar to that of the cultures living in mainland Siberia at the time. Japanese hunter-gatherer technology also resembled that used by people at the Ushki site in Kamchatka more than thirteen thousand years ago. Clearly, people moved north along the Pacific Rim using maritime technology. This is an important fact because it is necessary to show such an adaptation if we are going to assume that these people continued to move east from Kamchatka along the coast of the Aleutian Islands of Alaska just before or even during the height of the Last Glacial Maximum, twenty-five thousand years ago or so.

Pacific Rim Archaeology of the Americas

Archaeological data reveal that hunter-gatherer-fishers had a small maritime presence in the northern Pacific Rim region by twenty-five thousand years ago. More research needs to be conducted along the submerged Kamchatkan coastline to find early sites to match those in Japan, but people likely lived in Kamchatka by that time. This population likely split in two, with some moving north along the Beringian coastline and another group pushing east along the ice sheets that encompassed the many scattered islands of the Aleutian Island archipelago. Evidence in the Aleutian Islands

While archaeological evidence in the area remains scarce, Beringian hunters traveling by sea likely would have passed through the Aleutian Islands, seen here in this US Navy photograph from the mid-twentieth century taken near Unalaska. Library of Congress

is scant for this period, but Beringian populations almost certainly traveled by this route.

The sea ice twenty-five thousand years ago was likely a significant deterrent to migration through the Aleutians, but that doesn't mean it was impossible. The sea ice was likely scattered with pockets of exposed land along the Pacific Coast of Alaska, so archaeologists are trying to find those land exposures today in an attempt to identify landforms that may have been used by early people on the Pacific Coast of Alaska and points south. Consider that shorelines at the time were significantly further—hundreds of feet perhaps—from the modern coast, meaning that archaeologists will likely need to use underwater archaeology to help identify early sites.

On-Your-Knees Cave, Alaska

One of the earliest coastal sites in Alaska is On-Your-Knees Cave on Prince of Wales Island. Dated to a bit more than ten thousand years ago, it is quite young compared to the previously mentioned sites in Beringia, Japan, and Kamchatka. Nevertheless, archaeological and genetic data from On-Your-Knees Cave are important for establishing a Pacific Rim human population at the end of the LGM. People who lived at the site utilized a typical Denali Complex toolkit, which was mostly comprised of microblades but also included bifacial tools. This toolkit resembles those used in both eastern and western Beringia during the LGM.

Archaeologists also discovered human skeletal remains at On-Your-Knees Cave. According to Washington State University professor Brian Kemp, these remains suggested a diet heavily based on maritime resources, likely involving offshore procurement of sea mammals, saltwater fish, and shellfish. These findings matter because they indicate a well-adapted human subsistence to maritime life along the Pacific Coast more than ten thousand years ago.

DNA analysis of the human skeletal remains from On-Your-Knees Cave show a D4 H3a haplogroup, identical to that of the Anzick boy, whose remains date to eleven thousand years ago in Montana (see chapter 3). This doesn't necessarily mean that the Anzick boy and early Montanans are directly descended from people that lived on the Alaska coast. But the similar DNA haplogroup does show that the Anzick boy and the individual from On-Your-Knees Cave share a common ancestor from the D4-H3a DNA haplogroup. This common ancestor likely derived from somewhere in eastern Beringia to the north, either on the coast or inland (or both). It is possible that some portion of that ancestral family migrated south through the interior route from interior Alaska to Montana, while still another group migrated south along the Pacific Coast to On-Your-Knees Cave on Prince of Wales Island. It is just as likely that the common ancestor moved from Beringia down the Pacific Coast. Some of those people may have remained on the coast in Alaska while another group pushed into the interior toward Montana. Either scenario is possible. So, the fact that the two skeletons—one in coastal Alaska and one in Montana—share an identical DNA haplogroup supports the possibility of both a Pacific Coast migration route and/or an inland route for the peopling of Montana.

Another important Pacific Rim site in the Americas is located on Calvert Island, British Columbia, about three hundred miles south of Prince of Wales Island and about fifty miles northwest of the city of Vancouver. One group of researchers found footprints on an ancient shoreline at the site. The shoreline was located six to ten feet lower than the modern one and dated to between fourteen thousand and eleven thousand years ago. Other areas along the coast showed ancient shorelines more than five hundred feet from the modern one. Researchers Duncan McLaren, Daryl Fedje, and Angela Dyck, among others, surveyed the lower, ancient shoreline and found twenty-nine human footprints from three different individuals walking along the beach more than thirteen thousand years ago. A subsequent publication by the group noted that the Pacific Coast likely also had refugia, or locations that supported human life, between glacial ice flows from nineteen thousand to sixteen thousand years ago, in the heart of the LGM. The refugia contained hospitable landforms, including plants and animals that could sustain a hunter-gatherer lifestyle. The presence of refugia makes the Pacific Coast an even more likely migration route than previously thought, as marine-adapted foragers could simply move from refugia to refugia along the coast to find places to camp and food to eat.

These two sites—On-Your-Knees Cave and Calvert Island—support the hypothesis that a well-adapted maritime hunter-gatherer-fisher culture existed on the northwest coast of North America just after the Last Glacial Maximum. While they are both only ten thousand to eleven thousand years old, the sites provide evidence of maritime adaptation in the region. Surely, this implies that people had lived there much longer. The two sites also indicate that land refugia were present along the coastline that would have helped support human populations moving south from Beringia during the LGM or soon thereafter.

Pre-Clovis Pacific Coast Sites that Support an Early Coastal Migration

In addition to the northwest coast sites, several early sites have been investigated along the Pacific Coast. While these are inland hunter-gatherer sites, they show that people were in the Americas before Clovis, over 11,500 years ago. The fact that these pre-Clovis sites are within a hundred miles or so of the Pacific Coast may support the hypothesis that early people migrated down the coast first then pushed into the interior. This is a point of significant debate among archaeologists, but the data seem to support the Pacific Coast route as the source of the earliest migration to the Americas. All of these sites predate twelve thousand years ago, making them at least one thousand years older than the theoretical opening of the Ice-Free Corridor. It makes sense, then, that many archaeologists believe that the Pacific Coast route was used first.

The rest of this chapter examines the key sites that show that early Americans were here before Clovis and likely migrated down the Pacific Coast. One of the sites—Arlington Springs in the Channel Islands of California—contains the oldest human remains ever found in North America. All of these sites support the contention that a maritime adaptation thrived among early Native Americans of the Pacific Coast of North America during the LGM.

Manis Mastodon, Washington

The Manis Mastodon site is located on the Olympic Peninsula south of the town of Sequim, Washington. In the 1970s, the Manis family found elephant tusks while excavating a pond on their property. The landowners called a group of archaeologists from Washington State University, including Professors Carl Gustafson and Richard Daugherty, to investigate. They excavated a nearly complete mastodon skeleton. Recent research by Michael Waters of Texas A&M University and Thomas Stafford of the University of Copenhagen, among several others, confirmed that the animal was killed by a bone projectile point, itself produced from mastodon bone. The archaeologists found the bone projectile point embedded in a rib on the back of the animal, likely indicating that it was attacked by human hunter-gatherers, who used atlatls to throw bone-tipped darts at the elephants.

The site is less than thirty to forty miles as the crow flies from the Pacific Coast, but it clearly indicates that a hunter-gatherer adaptation occurred around twelve thousand years ago. Data from the Manis Mastodon site support that from other near-coastal sites in suggesting that Late Pleistocene hunter-gatherer-fishers were not only adapted to a coastal, maritime way of life but also likely pushed into interior areas along major bays and rivers to hunt land mammals. Since the site is five hundred years older than the earliest Clovis sites, it also is among the sites that show the presence of people in the inland northwest of North America before Clovis.

Paisley Caves, Oregon

Another inland site from this period is Paisley Caves, Oregon, located about 125 miles east of Coos Bay and the Pacific Ocean. While Paisley Caves is located on a high and dry desert today, during the Late Pleistocene, more than twelve thousand years ago, the site was located on the shores of an ancient lake. Since that time, due to the warming climate, the ancient lakes have dried up. Prior to that, interior Oregon was rich in flora and fauna, making it a very productive landscape for early Native American hunter-gatherers.

Archaeologists from the University of Oregon, led by Dennis Jenkins, excavated the cave and recovered evidence of extensive human occupation dating back to the Late Pleistocene. Most importantly, researchers discovered coprolites, or fossilized waste, from a variety of animals, including humans and camels, dating to more than twelve thousand years ago. Along with the human coprolites, archaeologists found Western Stemmed projectile points, one of the earliest stone projectile points utilized by Native Americans in the Great Basin region of North America. People living at Paisley Caves hunted megafauna as well as smaller game such as rabbits.

They also collected an abundant array of wild plants such as bulrush to use in the production of textiles like clothing, basketry, and sandals.

Cooper's Ferry, Idaho

Another important inland site from this period is Cooper's Ferry in Idaho. This site, located along the upper reaches of the Salmon River, is one of the oldest archaeological sites in the interior northwest region. As with Paisley Caves, Cooper's Ferry yielded abundant evidence for use of the Western Stemmed projectile points between twelve thousand and thirteen thousand years ago. Archaeologists recovered evidence of not only the procurement of small- and medium-sized animals, such as rabbits and deer, but also the hunting of now-extinct horses that once lived in the area. A distinctive attribute of the stemmed projectile points at Cooper's Ferry is the serration along their edges, which resembles those found along the coast of California in the Channel Islands. The Western Stemmed points are very similar in their shape and size to those described earlier for the Ushki Site in Kamchatka, as well as stemmed points found at Late Pleistocene sites in Japan. While the presence of similar projectile points doesn't necessarily connect the sites culturally, it shows that their subsistence systems were similar enough that they had adapted identical hunting technologies on both sides of the Pacific Rim. Given what we know about human migrations along the Pacific Rim, the similar technologies likely share some degree of ancestry as well.

Channel Islands, California

The California coastline has yielded numerous sites along ancient shorelines indicating that ancient hunter-gatherers had a well-adapted maritime subsistence system more than twelve thousand years ago. At the Arlington Springs site, located on Santa Rosa Island within the Channel Islands, archaeologists recovered the oldest human remains ever found on the Pacific Coast. These remains date to eleven thousand years ago—the same age as charcoal recovered at the site—and reflect isotopic data similar to that identified at the On-Your-Knees Cave site in Alaska, namely reflecting a diet reliant exclusively on marine life. In fact, the Channel Islands contain the first North American sites showing that ancient Pacific Rim peoples used boats in their daily lives. While the Channel Islands sites are not pre-Clovis, they indicate that people had adapted to a maritime culture by around eleven thousand years ago and used technology that looked nothing like Clovis. The fact that people used boats and had a well-adapted maritime lifestyle certainly suggests that humans had lived near the Pacific Coast of California earlier than eleven thousand years ago.

Even with the lower ocean levels of the Late Pleistocene, travel from the mainland California coast to Santa Rosa Island necessitated an ocean voyage of at least thirty miles. Similarly, another site, Daisy Cave, excavated by University of Oregon archaeologist Jon Erlandson and his colleagues, identified a vast array of maritime foods used by early Native Americans on the California coast. They also uncovered eleven-thousand-year-old fishing lures, twine sandals, and sea grass baskets, not to mention remains from eighteen different species of fish. The earliest radiocarbon date at the site is more than fifteen thousand years ago. The stemmed projectile points found at Daisy Cave and other California coastal sites are similar to the Western Stemmed varieties found at Paisley Caves and Cooper's Ferry. However, the coastal California points have a distinctive curved blade with serrations (rather than the straight blade found at the interior sites) perhaps adapted for maritime fishing and hunting. In addition, these California sites yielded a large variety of crescents used in the butchery of sea life procured from the Pacific Ocean.

Sites in the American Southwest

Two archaeological sites in the American Southwest support the presence of people in the Americas before Clovis, as well as the likely use of a Pacific Coast migration. These sites—the Buttermilk Complex (Texas) and White Sands (New Mexico)—both date significantly earlier than the opening of the inland corridor around twelve thousand years ago. Further, each contains evidence suggesting that early Native Americans migrated along the Pacific Coast before moving into the interior of the continent once they reached the warmer climates of what is now the southwestern United States.

Originally interpreted as very early Clovis-age sites, the Gault and Debra Friedkin sites—aka the Buttermilk Complex—have yielded well-dated, stratified archaeological deposits dating back as early as fifteen thousand years ago. The sites are located along the terraces of Buttermilk Creek in central Texas. The Gault site yielded stemmed projectile points somewhat similar to those found in California, Idaho, and Oregon that predate Clovis. This is the first site to have stratified deposits showing that the stemmed projectile points were used by Native Americans living in the western United States pre-Clovis.

Finally, we return to the footprints of people found dating to more than twenty thousand years ago in White Sands National Park, New Mexico. Dozens of footprints from multiple individuals have been preserved at the site, with radiocarbon-dated seeds placing their age at more than twenty-three thousand years ago. Even if the site dates to only twelve thousand or

Footprints found at White Sands National Park, New Mexico, seen in this National Park Service photograph, may indicate that the earliest Native Americans lived there more than twenty thousand years ago. Such a discovery, if the age is proven accurate, will rewrite the timeline of human migration to the Americas.

Courtesy of the National Park Service

thirteen thousand years ago—taking the reservoir effect, in which organic materials from maritime environments produce artificially early radiocarbon dates, into account—this area of New Mexico was probably similar to the region of Buttermilk Creek in Texas. While White Sands is a desert today, the Tularosa Basin was more humid and contained abundant vegetation, including large expanses of grasslands that supported large herds of mammoths, camels, horses, and sloths.

The White Sands footprints site is more than eight thousand years older than any of the other very early North American sites discussed in this chapter. As a result, the White Sands footprints will come under even more intensive scrutiny from modern archaeologists. If the footprints hold up to that scrutiny, it most certainly points to the migration of people from Beringia before the LGM, more than twenty-five thousand years ago, or at least down the Pacific Coast during the very early portion of the LGM. Even though the footprints may date to only thirteen thousand years ago, they still place humans in New Mexico well before Clovis and earlier than the proposed opening of the Ice-Free Corridor, confirming that people used the Pacific Coast as their earliest migration route.

Given their extreme distance from Montana, we won't spend much time on the sites south of the US-Mexico border. But several sites in Central and South America indicate a human presence along the coast as well as in the interior that dates as far back as 12,500 years ago, if not longer. The most important of these sites is Monte Verde in Chile. The site is located on a river terrace more than thirty miles from the Pacific Ocean. The site yielded ancient living structures, stone tools, leather fragments, and plant remains dated to around 12,500 years ago, making it one of the oldest sites anywhere in North or South America. Monte Verde offers unique insight into the peopling of the Americas given that it is located at the far southern tip of South America. It supports the Pacific Coast migration model and shows that people must have migrated north-to-south along the coast during the Last Glacial Maximum of the Late Pleistocene. If people were living in Chile 12,500 years ago, they must have started their migration south from Beringia significantly earlier.

Conclusion

So what does all of this have to do with Montana's first peoples? First, the presence of several archaeological sites that are more than twelve thousand years old in the western portion of the Americas proves that the first people on either continent arrived before the Clovis culture developed in North America. In addition, if the Ice-Free Corridor didn't open until after twelve thousand years ago, these older sites in the western Americas indicate that the earliest migrations followed the kelp highway down the Pacific Coast. Further, sites along and near the Pacific Coast bear earlier dates than those of the interior, and geological studies indicate that the coastal route was ice-free significantly earlier than the inland route. Given this, the coastal migration route is a viable contender to be the migration route taken by the first Montanans. In this scenario, the first Americans migrated south along the Pacific Coast from Beringia and then moved inland along river corridors—such as the Snake, Columbia, and Salmon—into interior North America, including Montana.

The Pacific Coast migration occurred sometime after fifteen thousand years ago and likely continued in multiple migration waves after that time. Whether the migration occurred before twenty-three thousand years ago is another question. The only site that is potentially that old is White Sands in New Mexico. Other sites in Alaska, British Columbia, Washington, Oregon, California, Texas, and South America date to between twelve thousand and thirteen thousand years ago. In contrast, the Anzick site in Montana is only eleven thousand years old.

Sites in western North America such as Manis Mastodon and Paisley Caves start to show an inland adaptation for early hunter-gatherers around thirteen thousand years ago or so. Similarly, the Cooper's Ferry site in Idaho indicates that early Native Americans migrated from the coast to the interior of North America, using Western Stemmed projectile points, to hunt a variety of animals in the upper reaches of the Salmon River. Also around thirteen thousand years ago, people lived comfortably within fifteen miles of Grangeville, Idaho, only one hundred miles west of the Montana-Idaho state line.

The presence of interior-adapted hunter-gatherers in Idaho at this early date suggests that they could have easily continued west into the Bitterroot Valley of Montana. Today, the route from Grangeville, Idaho, to Missoula, Montana, crosses a well-established Native American trail at Lolo Pass. This may have been the original route used by the earliest Indigenous peoples to get to Montana.

Other possible interior migration routes include the Clark Fork River valley, which joins the Columbia River, to Missoula, Montana, in the east. However, as the next chapter discusses at length, this region along the Clark Fork was the drainage corridor for Glacial Lake Missoula around thirteen thousand years ago. So far, archaeological data indicate that people were not present in this region at that time.

Another route of early hunter-gatherer migration could have been the

Snake River valley, which winds its way through Idaho and Wyoming into the southern reaches of Yellowstone National Park. However, glaciers that measured hundreds of feet high likely blocked this migration route until after thirteen thousand years ago or later. The high-elevation Yellowstone Plateau was covered by a significant ice cap during the last glaciation. That would have likely prevented northward migration from the Snake River valley into Montana until after that time.

The next chapter will look at Great Plains and Rocky Mountain archaeological sites in Montana and beyond to see if the first people to Montana could have used the inland corridor of Canada instead of traveling along the coast and then following major river valleys eastward into the interior. There is still abundant controversy regarding which migration route humans used first: coastal, inland, or some combination of the two. The archaeological community largely agrees that the data presented in this chapter indicate that people were in the Americas before Clovis. However, whether those data show that people migrated down the coast first is murkier. Remember that the earliest Pacific Coast sites show human occupation only by around eleven thousand years ago. Most archaeologists that support the Pacific Coast migration have taken a leap of faith, so to speak, that earlier sites were either inundated by the rising sea levels after thirteen thousand years ago or simply exist undiscovered along the coast. There is much future research that needs to be done to explore underwater sites along the Pacific Coast; as of now, many archaeologists remain skeptical of the early Pacific Coast route. With that in mind, let's discuss the alternative hypothesis: the inland Ice-Free Corridor.

✷

CHAPTER SIX

Migration through the Rockies

The end of the last chapter proposed that the first Montanans might have arrived in the Big Sky State via the Pacific Coast and then by traveling east along inland waterways such as the Columbia, Snake, Salmon, and Clark Fork Rivers. This timeline makes sense for a migration of inland-adapted hunter-gatherers in the Late Pleistocene, at least in terms of the timing of the opening of glacial ice sheets along the coast and the migration of people along the Pacific Rim and subsequently through river valleys to Montana between twenty-three thousand and twelve thousand years ago.

However, there are two reasons to be somewhat skeptical of this proposed migration timeline for the earliest Native Americans to Montana. First, while it suggests that the earliest archaeological sites in Montana would exist in the far western portion of the state, no very early sites have been found in far western Montana along the proposed migration routes. Second, the Western Stemmed projectile points used by people at Cooper's Ferry, Idaho, thirteen thousand years ago, and at Paisley Caves, Oregon, after twelve thousand years ago, do not match the technology of the early Native Americans discovered in Montana so far. The earliest sites in Montana—such as the famous Anzick site in Wilsall—indicate a reliance on Clovis technology for subsistence.

While many archaeologists believe that the cultures that used the Western Stemmed points in the far western and southwestern United States preceded Clovis as the first people in the Americas, the Clovis culture may still have been first in Montana and much of the Rocky Mountains and Great Plains regions of the interior United States. So, if the Pacific Coast migration route doesn't explain how Native Americans arrived in Montana, then how did they get here? Did early Native American hunter-gatherers stop their migration to the interior northwest due to the Bitterroot Mountains that lay in between the Salmon River and Montana? Did hunter-gatherers not want to cross the daunting Lolo and Lookout mountain passes on the Idaho-Montana border?

Did Glacial Lake Missoula Stop Eastward Migration?

Living in Missoula, Montana, I can just look out the window of my house and see the ripple marks from the former glacial lake that filled the city more than thirteen thousand years ago. The Laurentide Ice Sheet reached just north of the city, with meltwater from the glacier forming a gigantic glacial lake that spanned hundreds of square miles of the Missoula Valley, reaching all the way to Drummond, some fifty miles east. Geologists suggest that the large glacial lake melted and drained periodically during a several-hundred-year period at the end of the Late Pleistocene. The lake was completely drained by about the time the first hunter-gatherers might have ventured into the region, approximately thirteen thousand years ago.

Before it emptied completely, however, the lake drained multiple times from its source in the Missoula Valley through the Clark Fork River valley and, ultimately, into the famous channeled scablands of eastern Washington. It is unlikely that the first people to Montana witnessed the flooding and emptying of Glacial Lake Missoula. Archaeologists have never identified archaeological sites in any areas around the ancient shorelines of the glacial lake. There are also no sites dating to earlier than twelve thousand years ago in eastern Washington or northern Idaho. The earliest sites in Montana—even the Lindsay Mammoth site, which dates to 12,300 years ago—postdate the last draining of the lake. While early Native American hunter-gatherers likely had populated the Pacific Coast and even some interior areas such as the Salmon River valley, we have no evidence that they continued east into Montana.

Two significant geographic obstacles—the Bitterroot Mountains and Glacial Lake Missoula—posed a challenge for those attempting to migrate beyond the Salmon River thirteen thousand years ago or so. It certainly would have been a daunting landscape for hunter-gatherers and may have stalled eastward travel. Is this why we don't find any sites that date earlier than twelve thousand years ago or so in Montana? Was the route to Montana blocked not only by the Ice-Free Corridor but also by the flood-scavenged valleys and glacial lakes of western Montana until after thirteen thousand years ago?

While it's intriguing to think that the first Montanans sat along the shores of Glacial Lake Missoula, it instead looks like the first Native Americans arrived several hundred years after the lake was gone. However, future archaeological research in western Montana could prove this assumption to be wrong.

So, what do we know about the earliest archaeological sites in Montana? This chapter will look at early sites in places like Montana, Alberta, and Wyoming. It examines whether the first people to Montana could have traveled along the inland corridor along the Rocky Mountain Front of Canada.

Up until the 1990s, archaeologists were unsure as to which route—inland or coastal—the first people to the Americas used. At that time, Clovis was thought to have been the first Native American culture at around 11,500 years ago. Since the 1990s, archaeologists have discovered numerous sites along the Pacific Coast and in the western and southwestern United States (see the last chapter) that significantly predate Clovis as the first cultures in North and South America. One only needs to compare the dates of these early western North and South American sites with the dates for the opening of the Ice-Free Corridor to eliminate that route as the source of the earliest human migrations south into North America. Even if you take into consideration the Monte Verde site in Chile, which dates to more than thirteen thousand years ago, it would have been impossible for the first Native Americans to have used the inland corridor to get there.

Geography and Opening Timeline of the Ice-Free Corridor

While the first people to arrive in the Americas did not migrate through the Ice-Free Corridor, it could have been used by the first people to travel to the Americas east of the Rockies, including Montana. The coastal Cordilleran and the inland Laurentide Ice Sheets coalesced across Canada and well into what is today Alaska during the Last Glacial Maximum (LGM). Roughly fifteen thousand years ago, the coastal melting of glaciers on the Cordilleran ice sheet began. The Laurentide Ice Sheet likely continued intact, with localized melting in warmer sections, until approximately thirteen thousand years ago. Along the Pacific, glaciers melted more quickly due to their proximity to ocean waters, but there was no such relief for the inland Laurentide Ice Sheet. Current geological and paleo-botanical data indicate that the Ice-Free Corridor was not open to humans, plants, and animals until after thirteen thousand years ago.

Geologist and archaeologist David Palacios wrote in 2020 that it has been extremely difficult to evaluate when the Ice-Free Corridor opened and became biologically viable, or traversable by animals, plants, and humans. However, 2017 research by University of Alberta professor Duane Froese and several colleagues indicates that bison were present within the corridor thirteen thousand years ago. Their study, published in the *Proceedings of the National Academy of Sciences* (PNAS), examined seventy-eight bison fossils from Beringia and inland North America, including forty-nine from the region of the Ice-Free Corridor. Genetic analysis of the bison fossils indicated that herds from Beringia, north of the Laurentide Ice Sheet, were distinct from bison found at the same time south of the ice sheet in southern

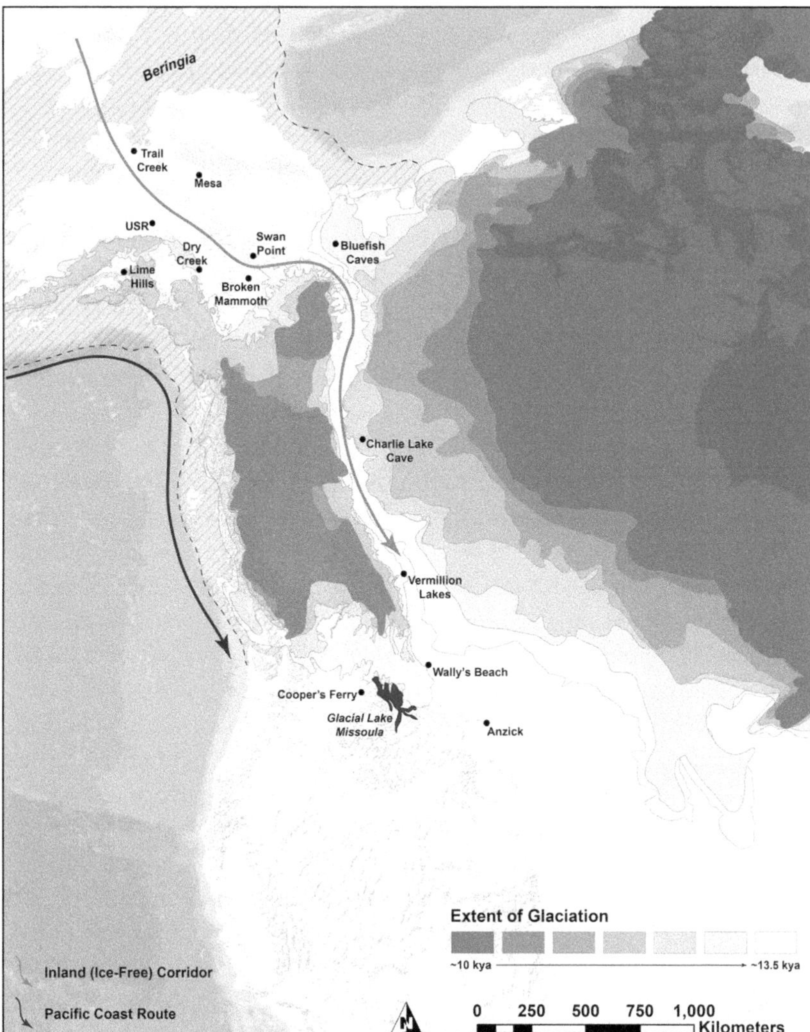

This map points out several important archaeological sites in relation to Beringia and the Ice-Free Corridor as well as key interior sites south of the inland corridor. Monte White

Canada and Montana. Thirteen thousand years ago, however, the two herds appear to have blended, indicative of the opening of the Ice-Free Corridor for migration by animals. Their study indicated that southern bison started to move north as early as 13,400 years ago, with the melting of the Laurentide Ice Sheet along its southern border. As melting progressed, bison herds continued to push north and south respectively, until they merged.

The Ice-Free Corridor developed along the eastern front of the Canadian Rocky Mountains. The corridor appears to have been biologically viable thirteen thousand years ago, meaning that plants, animals, and humans could have lived in the region. While the corridor may have been open even earlier, post-glacial landscapes are filled with wetlands, rocky terrain, mosquitos, and settings not conducive for humans or other animals.

Alaskan Archaeological Sites Near the Ice-Free Corridor

While glaciers covered much of Alaska during the LGM, many interior river valleys remained ice-free north and west of the Laurentide Ice Sheet, allowing humans to move into the region. Several important archaeological sites north, south, and within the corridor—Swan Point, Bluefish Caves, and Upward Sun River—offer insight into when people might have traveled south into the Americas.

Swan Point shows a distinctive Beringian toolkit, similar to those used by people living in Siberia to the west. Dated to around twelve thousand years ago, Swan Point shows human movement into interior Alaska—eastern Beringia—just before the opening of the Ice-Free Corridor. People hunted swans, geese, and moose at the site and used obsidian found at Wrangell Mountain, which is located south of the site on the way to the Pacific Coast. The presence of this obsidian may show that interior-adapted Beringians migrated between the coast and the interior to procure seasonally available resources. Alternatively, it may show that coastal hunter-gatherers occasionally moved inland to hunt land mammals, such as caribou, stopping to collect obsidian from Wrangell Mountain during the journey. Or both scenarios could be true. Regardless, this evidence supports the contention, discussed earlier in this book, that people living on the coast and the interior were aware of each other and likely had significant cultural ties. It might even be possible that the people living in both regions were the same people, simply moving seasonally between the interior and the coast to exploit the available resources, including land mammals on the interior and marine mammals and fish resources on the coast.

Chapter 2 discussed Bluefish Caves in the Yukon, where archaeologists found a cut bone that dates as early as fifteen thousand years ago. While still controversial, this site suggests the potential of many others like it in Alaska. In terms of stone tool technology, these Alaskan sites share similar characteristics with sites in western Beringia. Anthropologist E. James Dixon has referred to this as the Paleoarctic Tradition. In Russia, the toolkit is referred to as the Dyuktai Culture, named after an important site there. In Alaska, it has often been referred to as the Denali Complex. Regardless of the name—Dyuktai, Denali, or Paleoarctic—all of these sites show the use of microblades manufactured from wedge-shaped cores to tip projectile points. Assorted bifacial tools also appear in the toolkits of some sites, with caribou hunting appearing to be a preferred subsistence strategy at the inland sites. However, early hunter-gatherers in Alaska used a variety of the region's foods, including all manner of small, medium, and large game, as well as birds and fish. Rather than an exclusive big-game hunting focus, interior Alaska Beringians were adapted to a well-balanced diet that exploited all available resources of the woodlands and river valleys of the region.

The interior valleys of Alaska contain numerous sites from this period. While the Upward Sun River site dates to only ten thousand years ago or so, DNA data from the human skeletal remains found there show that the individuals buried at the site descended from a more ancient Beringian population. Upward Sun River also contained bone and antler rods as well as numerous large bifaces that perhaps show links with the southern Clovis culture.

In addition to Swan Point, Bluefish Caves, and Upward Sun River, important inland Alaska sites include Broken Mammoth, Lime Hills Cave, Trail Creek Caves, and several sites in the Nenana River valley. These sites are located northwest of the opening for the Ice-Free Corridor. They show that people were in an excellent geographic position to take advantage of the opening of the corridor and potentially move south to Montana as early as twelve thousand years ago or so.

The Trail Creek Caves site is located in western Alaska within a series of caves and hills that rise to the east above the Bering Strait, within what is today called Bering Land Bridge National Preserve on the Seward Peninsula. Originally found in 1928, Danish archaeologists excavated the site in the 1940s before the National Park Service did the same in the 1980s. The NPS archaeologists identified bison bone dated to more than thirteen thousand years ago as well as a horse scapula dated to nearly sixteen thousand years ago; however, evidence that people were at these two sites during that time is likely nonexistent. The earliest evidence connecting humans to the site are Denali Complex (or Dyuktai) artifacts, including microblades, a slotted antler spearhead, wedge-shaped cores, and a single biface. These artifacts are similar to those used at sites in western Beringia.

The antler spear tip recovered at the site is an excellent example of how Beringian hunters hafted microblades for use as projectiles. They placed the small linear blades within slots engraved on the side of long, narrow antler spear tips, likely glued with any number of natural binders, including blood and tree sap. The microblade inserts functioned well for the killing of caribou, as the row of multiple small blades sliced through the animals with ease.

DNA analysis revealed that human skeletal remains found at Trail Creek Caves dated to about nine thousand years ago, indicating a strong connection to the individuals found at Upward Sun River. The human remains from these two sites show that a widespread Beringian population existed in the region during the Late Pleistocene.

The Lime Hills site in interior Alaska is another location with archaeological remains dating to more than ten thousand years ago. This site is located on a high hill above the Stony River, which flows north and east into Cook Inlet of the Pacific Ocean approximately forty miles east of the site. Alaska's largest city, Anchorage, is also located on Cook Inlet some eighty miles east of the site. Professor Robert Ackerman of Washington State University and his students recovered caribou remains with cut marks possibly made by humans that dated to 15,690 years ago, as well as a tool that was likely used as a hide scraper more than 13,000 years ago. While those dates and the involvement of humans at the site are debatable, the team also dated Denali Complex microblades at the site to 9,500 years ago.

Two hundred miles northeast of the Lime Hills as the crow flies, the Nenana and Tanana River valleys of interior Alaska have yielded dozens of archaeological sites, with several showing evidence of human occupation dating to the LGM, including the Broken Mammoth and Dry Creek Cave sites. Interestingly, these two sites contain evidence of Denali Complex artifacts, including microblades and wedge-shaped cores, but also an increasing number of bifacial tools, the presence of which is a hallmark of the Clovis culture.

Another site near the Dry Creek and Broken Mammoth sites is Upward Sun River, which also yielded several bifaces. That site also included bone and antler rods eerily similar to those found at the Anzick site in Montana. Collectively, these three sites in interior Alaska support the contention that pre-Clovis cultures adopted bifacial technology. These sites reveal technological similarities that potentially link the cultures of interior Alaska with Clovis cultures that emerged south of the ice sheets around eleven thousand years ago.

The Dry Creek site along the Nenana River and the Broken Mammoth site along the Tanana River are two more of the important Alaskan sites that may link LGM cultures of Alaska with the Clovis cultures of Montana. The Dry Creek site yielded evidence of two human occupations of the area, the first revealing use of bifaces, scrapers, and large blades to kill and butcher Dall sheep and elk around 11,120 years ago. The second shows that humans used bifaces and Denali Complex microblades around 10,700 years ago. Importantly, archaeologists at the sites found that bifaces were significant technological attributes in both cases, including those that are characteristic of the Beringian Denali/Dyuktai (Paleoarctic) complexes. It appears that hunter-gatherers had developed and frequently used biface technology in interior Alaska. Were these hunter-gatherers the people that subsequently moved south through the Ice-Free Corridor to Montana?

The Broken Mammoth site, located on a high ridge overlooking the Tanana River of central Alaska, also yielded evidence that might show a north-south connection. Similar to Dry Creek, Broken Mammoth contained two main occupations. The earliest zone dated from 11,300 to 11,700 years ago and contained bifaces, scrapers, and microblades. The next occupation dated to about 10,500 years ago and contained bifaces, scrapers, and a very

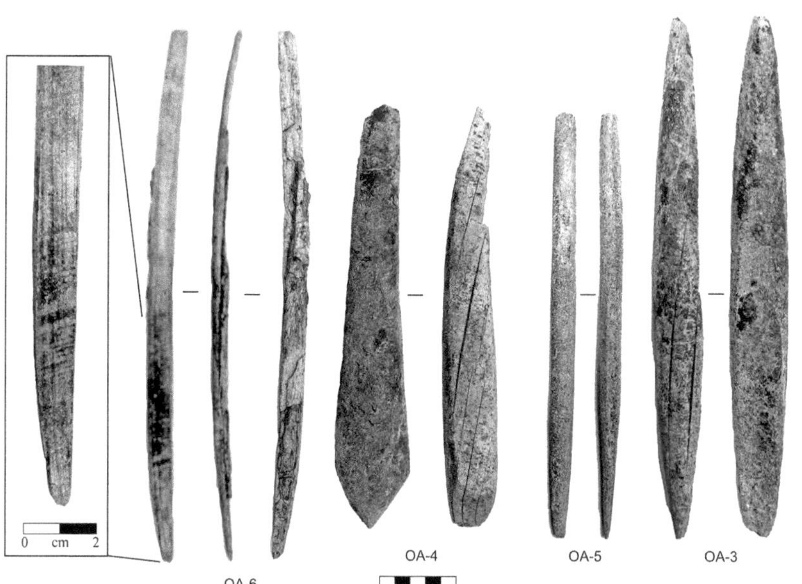

Late Pleistocene hunters in Siberia and North America, including people who lived at the Anzick site in Montana, used ivory rods similar to these artifacts found at the Broken Mammoth site in Alaska. C. Holmes photograph, courtesy of Kathryn E. Krasinski

rare bone needle. This occupation also had a projectile point with a concave base very similar in morphology to the lanceolate projectile points used by early Native Americans south of the ice sheets.

A unique ivory tool ranks as one of the most interesting finds at Broken Mammoth. This tool, which was carved into a curved, linear form and likely functioned as either a projectile point or a foreshaft to a projectile point, closely resembles bone rods found at several other sites in Beringia, including the Upward Sun River and Holzman sites in Alaska, the Yana RHS site in Siberia, and even the Anzick site in Montana, among others. It is fascinating to think that the stone and bone technology used more than twenty-five thousand years ago in Siberia continued to dominate Paleoindian lifestyles until at least eleven thousand years ago in Montana.

Yet another Alaskan site provides evidence that people migrated north from Montana and its vicinity into Alaska. Just as this occurred among bison herds, it appears to have also been the case for people. One of the hallmark characteristics of Clovis cultures is the presence of distinctive projectile points. Clovis points are produced via a unique technology called fluting, in which a flake is removed from the concave base of the projectile point. This flute in the concave base facilitates hafting into a foreshaft. Clovis sites in Montana and the rest of the northern Great Plains, as discussed later in this book, date to around eleven thousand years ago, if not a bit earlier. However, two sites in Alaska show evidence of fluting around ten thousand years ago. The fluting technology innovated by Clovis appears to have migrated north into Alaska. While the fluting of projectile points in Alaska is not identical to that used by Clovis people in places like Montana, it is similar enough to assume that it was derivative of the original Clovis technology as it traveled back through the corridor into Alaska.

The Mesa site in northern Alaska, located above the Brooks Range, yielded large lanceolate points like those used by Great Plains hunter-gatherers after 11,000 years ago. One of the large bifaces from the site showed evidence of fluting as well. The Putu site also yielded several projectile points with fluting but has radiocarbon dates of around 9,000 to 10,000 years ago. Finally, Jeff Rasic of Gates of the Arctic National Park has conducted excavations at another Alaska site—Raven Bluff along the Kivalina River—that date to about 10,100 years ago. Rasic and his colleagues recovered fluted projectile points side-by-side with microblades and evidence of extensive caribou hunting. It appears, then, that Clovis people south of the ice sheets invented the fluting of projectile points and that the technology, much like the bison, spread north through Canada into the wide-open river valleys of interior Alaska.

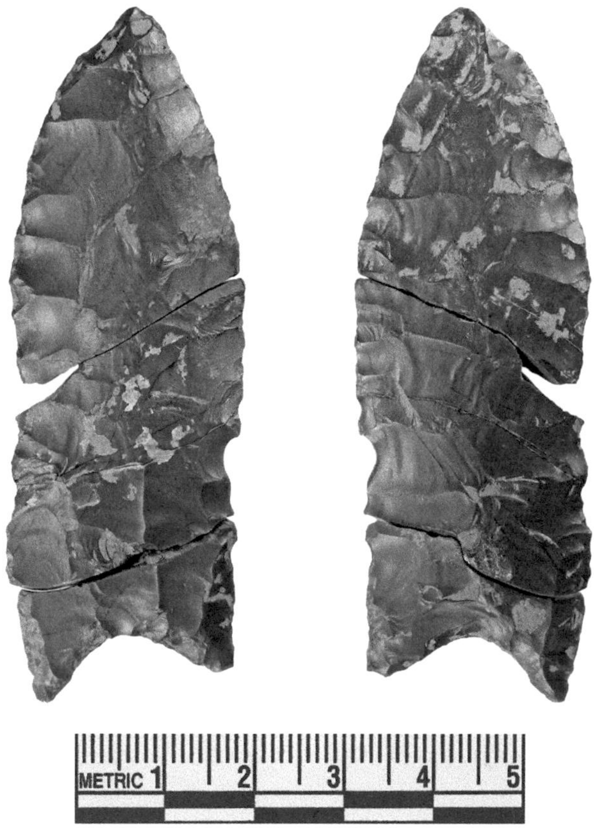

While Clovis people, who lived in Montana and throughout North America, invented them, fluted projectile points migrated northward into Alaska with hunters. Archaeologists found these points, which date to around ten thousand years ago, at the Raven Bluff site in Alaska. Jeffrey Rasic photograph

So, the fossil data show that while significant numbers of bison moved north, large numbers of bison also moved south through the melting Ice-Free Corridor in Alaska. In addition, the archaeological site data appear to show that incipient Paleoindian technology—bifaces and bone rods—were used in Alaska and may have moved south to places like Montana where the Clovis cultures adapted them. The Ice-Free Corridor, once opened, was a new territory, and people and animals exploited it from both ends of the ice sheets.

Early Sites in the Ice-Free Corridor of Canada

Given the awful conditions of the Ice-Free Corridor of Canada at the end of the LGM, thirteen thousand years ago, it makes sense that archaeologists haven't found much evidence of people living there. Though the corridor would have been rife with rock, muck, and water—not to mention mosquitoes—bison, grasses, and plants likely appeared in some but not all sections. Given the dearth of archaeological sites in the corridor, it appears that people may have moved through it to find wider and greener pastures filled with game in places like Montana. On the other hand, the human presence in the corridor could be unrecognized, having diminished due to poor soil conditions. There may have been a substantial push of people through the corridor from Alaska, but water, dirt, and wind may have destroyed the archaeological sites left by these intrepid Beringians moving south.

Imagine a family venturing into this unexplored region south of their homeland in Alaska and camping on a high terrace above a river near the output flow of a glacier. While the scenery likely would have been incredible, with glacial waterfalls flowing from massive glaciers to the east and west, it would have been cold, wet, and miserable, night after night. Why, they might ask, did we leave Alaska for this? They would have been shivering and likely hungry. And don't forget the mosquitoes.

After having spent the night in that beautiful spot, the family would have left early in the morning, leaving scant evidence of their camp. Even if they built a fire, killed and butchered a bison or caribou, outwash flows of water from the nearby glaciers might have swept through the valley and removed any evidence of the camp the next spring. Archaeologists looking for such a camp would not find it. They might find a stone tool or two, maybe a piece of fire-cracked rock from the fire, or perhaps nothing at all.

In fact, only three significant sites have been excavated within the corridor, and one is potentially an early Clovis-related site. Archaeologists discovered the first two sites—Charlie Lake Cave and Vermillion Lakes—in the central portion of the corridor, within the Canadian provinces of Alberta and British Columbia, respectively. The Vermillion Lakes site, located on the Bow River near Calgary, yielded radiocarbon dates of about 10,500 years ago. Stone tools at the site resemble those found at the Putu and Mesa sites in Alaska and artifacts more often uncovered at sites in Montana and its vicinity. Vermillion Lakes, then, is another site that shows the diffusion of people or technology from south-to-north through the Ice-Free Corridor to Alaska.

Similarly, Charlie Lake Cave near Banff contained fluted projectile points with concave bases as well as Paleoindian-like scrapers and blades

Human migration through the Ice-Free Corridor occurred in landscapes similar to the ones found in the modern northern Rocky Mountains in places such as Banff, Canada, as seen in this photograph. Author photograph

more typically found at sites to the south. With radiocarbon dates of 10,800 years ago, the site likely also shows south-to-north movements of people from the Great Plains of North America into Canada, probably following the bison herds that pushed north as well. People to the south used similar projectile points as early as 11,000 years ago.

The Original Clovis Site?

Finally, there's Wally's Beach, an archaeological site near Medicine Hat, Alberta. Wally's Beach is one of the most amazing archaeological sites in the northern Great Plains. Located only thirty miles north of the Montana state line, at the far southern end of the Ice-Free Corridor, the site yielded some of the earliest evidence of Clovis technology found anywhere in North America. Led by Brian Kooyman, a team of archaeologists from the University of Calgary recovered abundant evidence that people living at the site hunted megafauna and used Clovis points as early as 11,400 years ago.

People who migrated south from Alaska toward Montana starting thirteen thousand years ago might have ended up in Alberta just a few generations later. For instance, if a woman and her family started to migrate south from Swan Point, Dry Creek, or Broken Mammoth through the river valleys of central Alaska, her great-great grandchildren and their families might have made it all the way to Montana or at the very least Alberta. Perhaps one of those descendants was the inventor of the unique, fluted Clovis points. Imagine that family: one night after another, over hundreds of years,

Led by Brian Kooyman, researchers from the University of Calgary recovered abundant evidence for the hunting of megafauna as well as the use of Clovis points as early as 11,400 years ago at the Wally's Beach site in southern Alberta, Canada.

Brian Kooyman photograph

they camped out in these buggy, icy landscapes with an occasional bighorn sheep or bison to hunt.

Now imagine that family having pushed through the Ice-Free Corridor, perhaps after several months and years of southward migration looking for a place to live. Finally, in September, around 11,500 years ago, they find the grassy pastures of the northern Great Plains. The vast mountains of the Rockies are only visible as snowcapped reminders to the west, while rivers and grasslands surround the family in all other directions. These people might have been pretty happy. They could rest on the banks of a beautiful river, grasslands all around, and see literally thousands of bison, mammoths, camels, and horses just walking around. Imagine that those animals had never seen people before. Easy prey. Lots of food. A newcomer in this area might tilt his head back, put his feet in the flowing river, and place a piece of grass in his mouth. His ancestors had started on the path from Alaska down an ice-free pathway between two gigantic ice sheets that took hundreds of years of trudging through the mucky, mosquito-ridden corridor to Alberta, Montana, and beyond. People have now arrived in Montana. Finally.

✷

CHAPTER SEVEN

When Did People Arrive in Montana?

The earliest archaeological sites in eastern Beringia—including Swan Point, Broken Mammoth, Bluefish Caves—are located near the northern entrance of the Ice-Free Corridor and date to around the time of its opening. Sites within the corridor date to about 11,000 years ago or just after. Wally's Beach, just south of the opening, is the earliest of the group at 11,400 years old. Based on the archaeological data, it appears that Beringians may have started to push south through the corridor as new territory to hunt and gather opened. This makes perfect sense for a population of hunter-gatherers making their living off the land. Certainly, the Ice-Free Corridor would have been a foreign land; but, at the same time, it would have looked like these peoples' homelands, with similar flora and fauna eventually spreading into the corridor. It is conceivable that the first hunter-gatherers in the Ice-Free Corridor may not have known they were colonizing previously uninhabited areas. They were simply living their lives. In so doing, they may have gradually made their way to Montana.

This chapter examines the Wally's Beach site in Alberta and the Lindsay Mammoth site in Montana. It will briefly compare the archaeological results from Lindsay Mammoth, potentially one of the earliest archaeological sites in Montana, with the Schaefer and Hebior sites near Kenosha, Wisconsin, which are of a similar age and show human butchery of male Columbian mammoths. Comparing the archaeological data from the three sites can help determine whether early people traveled through the Ice-Free Corridor and were present in North America before the Clovis culture.

While most archaeologists accept Anzick, which dates to about eleven thousand years ago, as Montana's oldest site, some argue that the Lindsay Mammoth site is even older. At Lindsay, Montana State University archaeologists excavated a mammoth that radiocarbon dating suggested was

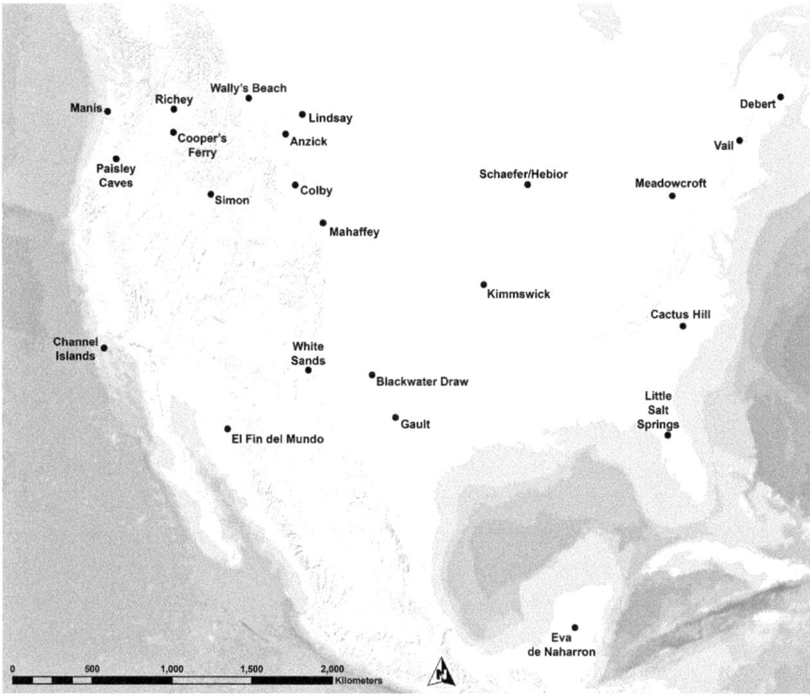

The Lindsay Mammoth and Wally's Beach sites—in Montana and Alberta, respectively—are among the earliest possible archaeological sites in North America. This map shows them in relation to similar findings across North America, including the Schaefer and Hebior sites in Wisconsin. Monte White

around twelve thousand years old. Lindsay Mammoth, however, is controversial. This chapter will discuss whether it qualifies as an archaeological or a paleontological site. The debate around the Lindsay Mammoth site revolves around one question: Did people kill and/or butcher the mammoth at the site twelve thousand years ago, or did the animal die of natural causes with no human predation?

Wally's Beach, Alberta

The Wally's Beach and Lindsay Mammoth sites are similar in one important aspect: archaeologists are not sure who or what killed the animals at these early sites in the northwestern Great Plains. For the purposes of this book, the Wally's Beach site is also relevant because it is located just north of the Montana state line, about thirty-five miles from the town of Babb on the Blackfeet Reservation.

As the end of the last chapter described, a team of archaeologists from the University of Calgary—including Brian Kooyman—analyzed the Wally's Beach site during the 2000s and 2010s. Kooyman, along with colleagues Michael Waters of Texas A&M University and Thomas Stafford of Aarhus University in Denmark, published their findings from Wally's Beach in the *Proceedings of the National Academy of Sciences* in 2015. Their paper notes that at the time of publication, Wally's Beach was the only site that contained "certain evidence for prehistoric human hunting of horse and camel in North America."

Wally's Beach is located on a high terrace, roughly one hundred feet above the nearby St. Mary River. In the early 2000s, the University of Calgary archaeologists identified Clovis points and evidence that those points were used to hunt musk oxen, caribou, camels, and bison. The original radiocarbon dates taken at the site—which placed its age at eleven thousand years old—supported Clovis occupation, much like the Anzick site.

Since those early discoveries, additional research in the 2010s revealed a bone bed comprised of seven butchered horses and one camel. Researchers found these animals with about thirty associated flaked stone tools that

At the Wally's Beach site in Alberta, archaeologists uncovered 11,400-year-old horse and camel remains, including the horse vertebrae pictured here. These animals were found with about thirty associated flaked stone tools that hunters used to process the animals. Brian Kooyman photograph

humans had used to process the animals. Unfortunately, the archaeologists have not yet determined which styles of projectile points people used at the site. While researchers found Clovis points that contained horse protein several hundred yards away from the bone bed, this evidence doesn't show beyond reasonable doubt that those Clovis points were used to kill the specific animals in the bone bed, just that the Clovis points had been used to kill or butcher horses at some point. Hopefully, technological advancements will allow us to determine whether Clovis or pre-Clovis hunters killed the horses and the camel. For now, it appears just as likely that people using non-Clovis technology killed the animals.

Waters, Stafford, and Kooyman conducted radiocarbon dating—taking twenty-seven separate dates—of the horses and camels and showed that they were all killed about 11,400 years ago. These dates would make Wally's Beach among the earliest Clovis sites. El Fin del Mundo, an elephant kill site in the Sonoran Desert of northern Mexico excavated by Guadalupe Sánchez and her colleagues from the Universidad Nacional Autónoma de México in Hermosillo, Sonora, yielded radiocarbon dates of about 11,500 years ago, placing it slightly earlier than the horse and camel kill site at Wally's Beach. Further, at El Fin del Mundo, Native Americans clearly used seven Clovis projectile points to kill two gomphotheres, a type of elephant with a smaller body than mammoths and mastodons that roamed Mexico in the Late Pleistocene.

In the conclusion to their important article about the findings at Wally's Beach, Kooyman, Waters, and their coauthors make a valuable distinction about the earliest archaeological sites on the northwestern Great Plains of Montana and Alberta: "We must realize that kill sites of this age will likely have very few artifacts in total. These few artifacts may be nondiagnostic and nonlithic; we should not necessarily expect to find a diagnostic artifact form." This is a crucial point to make about the evidence, or lack thereof, that the earliest North Americans left behind. Remember that the first people in the region may not have known the locations of good sources of stone. As David Meltzer of Texas A&M University notes in his book *First Peoples in a New World*, the earliest Native American hunter-gatherers needed to learn their landscape. It may have taken a few generations of living in the region for them to know the locations of stone they could use to make Clovis and other early projectile points.

So, what would these people have used to hunt and butcher their animals in the meantime? As we saw at the Manis Mastodon site in Washington State, it appears that the first Americans likely used bone, antler, and ivory to produce their hunting and butchery tools until they discovered the right varieties of stone. Eventually, they made the switch to stone projectile points produced from those lithic sources. At least three of the earliest sites in the region, all determined to be of pre-Clovis age—Wally's Beach, Manis Mastodon, and Paisley Caves—did not yield abundant evidence of stone tool use.

Schaefer and Hebior Mammoth Kills, Wisconsin

The Schaefer and Hebior Mammoth sites in Wisconsin, like Lindsay Mammoth site in Montana, are early mammoth kill sites in North America that lack significant stone tool assemblage. Yet archaeologists accept both as legitimate pre-Clovis sites.

Dan Joyce of the Kenosha Public Museum excavated the Schaefer Mammoth site in the early 1990s. The adult male mammoth remains were found on the edge of a pond in what had been a spruce forest during the Late Pleistocene. As with Lindsay, Schaefer was within several miles of the Laurentide Ice Sheet. Bone and wood found at the site helped date the mammoth to 12,500 years ago, well before Clovis. Archaeologists widely accept this site as valid due to the excessive evidence of human butchery, including the presence of stone tools used to process the animal.

Marquette University excavated the nearby Hebior Mammoth kill site later in the 1990s. This site also contained the remains of a male Columbian mammoth that dates to between 12,400 and 12,600 years old. As with Schaefer, this site yielded a very small number of stone tools, including a few stone flakes used to process the animal.

Neither Hebior nor Schaefer revealed evidence of the elephants' cause of death, so it is not clear whether human predation or natural causes led to their demise. However, based on the assemblage of stone tools at the sites and the butchery marks found on the mammoths, archaeologists are certain that people at the very least processed the animals. As a result, archaeologists consider these two sites to be among the earliest evidence that people left behind in North America.

The Lindsay Mammoth

That brings us to the Lindsay Mammoth site in Montana. The site was first identified in a farm field near the small eastern Montana town of Lindsay, roughly halfway between Circle and Glendive, in 1966. The following year, the landowners invited a team of archaeologists from Montana State University—led by George Arthur, a professor, and Leslie Davis, a University of Calgary graduate student—to excavate the site. Leslie Davis was well-known in Montana archaeological circles, having grown up in the Clark Fork valley west of Missoula, where he spent his time looking for Native

Researchers from Montana State University, some of whom can be seen in this Seiss Wagner photograph from the site, first excavated the Lindsay Mammoth site in 1967, revealing a single Columbian mammoth that likely died from natural causes. Many archaeologists question the evidence supporting a human presence at the site.
Courtesy of Museum of the Rockies, Bozeman

American artifacts in farm fields and river terraces. He went on to become one of the most important archaeologists ever to work in the state. Starting with the excavation at Lindsay, Davis conducted research at many of the most important Paleoindian archaeological sites in Montana.

At the Lindsay Mammoth site, Davis and his team excavated the remains of a single large mammoth, originally interpreted to be an imperial mammoth (*Mammuthus imperotor*). Since its original discovery, however, it has been reclassified as a Columbian mammoth (*Mammuthus columbi*), the same species found at the Schaefer and Hebior sites in Wisconsin. Columbian mammoths were the most common type of elephant found in Montana and vicinity during the Late Pleistocene. The team spent July and August of 1967 excavating the animal's remains. Based on wear patterns on its molars, the animal was determined to be about forty-five years old at the time of its death.

Located approximately seven miles northeast of the city of Glendive, the Lindsay Mammoth site would have sat only a few miles south of the Laurentide Ice Sheet during the Late Pleistocene, more than twelve thousand years ago. Early Native Americans in the region likely used the edges of the glacial margin as a geographic landmark and may not have ventured too far from it until they learned their way around the landscape. Several species of now-extinct megafauna—horses, camels, musk oxen, bison, and mammoths—lived along the glacial front in this part of present-day Montana during the Late Pleistocene. Christopher Hill from Boise State University has dated mammoth remains near Glendive and other areas of the lower Yellowstone River basin to more than twenty thousand years ago. So, when the first people arrived—perhaps as early as twelve thousand years ago—they found familiar animals, including the megafauna they hunted in the Ice-Free Corridor, along the Pacific Coast and further north in Beringia.

The first radiocarbon dates from the Lindsay Mammoth site, published in the 1980s, placed it to about 11,900 years old. In 1998, Leslie Davis and Christopher Hill, then Davis's colleague at Montana State, conducted additional radiocarbon dating that indicated an age of about 11,500 for the mammoth. In the early 2000s and 2010s, Hill and Davis conducted another round of radiocarbon dating using a mammoth rib that indicated the animal may have lived as long as 12,300 years ago. In a paper published in 2021, Thibaut Deviese from the radiocarbon lab at the University of Oxford in England, as well as a group of colleagues that included Thomas Stafford and Michael Waters, published a paper supporting this earlier date for the Lindsay Mammoth site.

Paleontologists were not able to determine a cause of death and found no evidence of human predation during the excavations of the mammoth. Davis, however, suggested that the stacking of parts of the mammoth's remains might indicate human butchering. He also identified the possible crushing of long bones for marrow extraction. Even if human hunters could not be proved to have killed the mammoth, could the animal have died a natural death but still have been scavenged by people? If so, the site would be similar to the Schaefer and Hebior sites in Wisconsin, which also showed that humans had butchered mammoths that died of natural causes more than twelve thousand years ago.

In his publications on the site, Davis contends that human butchery of the animal caused several bone fractures. He also reiterates that Native Americans stacked bone from the mammoth, placing two mammoth femurs on top of a pile of ribs. He says this could only have been done by people, not by natural causes. Davis also suggests hunters broke the mandible of the mammoth using a large sandstone block found at the site during excavations. They did so to get the fatty marrow in the center of the animal's bones.

However, Davis and his team from Montana State University did not find any additional evidence of the animal's cause of death. No stone tools were found among the bones either. For that reason, as with many of the sites in Alaska, such as Bluefish Caves, the association of humans with Lindsay Mammoth has long been the subject of debate.

Professor Kathryn Krasinski of Adelphi University in New York conducted one of the most important scientific analyses of the Lindsay Mammoth site for her doctoral dissertation at the University of Nevada, Reno, in 2010. During her research, Krasinski analyzed faunal remains (animal bone) from eight Clovis and pre-Clovis archaeological sites in North America, including Bluefish Caves in Alaska and Lindsay Mammoth. Her goal was to determine if the animal remains from those sites show evidence of a human presence; all of them had been received with skepticism due to a lack of stone tools or other obvious signs of people.

To determine if people killed and/or butchered the animals, Krasinski conducted bone modification experiments intended to show the distinct differences between human-produced butchery and cut marks and those produced naturally or by animals during predation. She then compared the results of her experiments to the faunal remains from these eight early sites.

Krasinski examined 276 individual bones from 74 elements (bone parts) of the Lindsay mammoth that now reside in the collections of the Museum of the Rockies in Bozeman. As with animal remains at all eight sites in her study, she noted the significant natural weathering of the animal's bones,

Archaeologists found the complete remains of a Columbian mammoth at the Lindsay site, including the massive leg bone shown in this Leslie B. Davis photograph.
Courtesy of Museum of the Rockies, Bozeman

which is not surprising given their great age. At Lindsay, as well as the other sites, she also noted that animals had gnawed and trampled the bones. This should be expected, since any large, deceased animal left out in the open plains of Montana twelve thousand years ago likely would have experienced some degree of animal predation. Wolves, bears, and cats, among many other smaller predators, were all present in Montana and likely would have taken advantage of the dead animal—whether humans were present or not—as an easy meal.

However, Krasinski also determined that the breakage patterns on a few of the larger bones may indicate the presence of humans. As she explains, "Lindsay material may have been modified by carnivores [but] potentially [also] by human free-throwing of boulders for marrow access." She notes the presence of the large sandstone blocks near the location of the marrow extraction as support for this interpretation. So, while people may not have killed the mammoth, hunter-gatherers may have encountered the dead animal and used large sandstone blocks to break open some of the larger bones to extract the marrow, a fatty and protein-rich food source harvested by hunter-gatherers across the world. Similar bone-marrow processing has been observed in some form at the Colby mammoth kill in Wyoming (see the next chapter), Wally's Beach, and the Schaefer and Hebior sites.

In addition to the bone breakage patterns indicating possible marrow extraction, Krasinski observed other marks on the bones that she believed human butchery left on the mammoth at Lindsay. She noted the presence of 346 marks on the Lindsay mammoth remains. She then examined these marks to determine the role of humans in the kill or butchery of the animal. Of the 346 marks, she found that 333 of them were due to natural causes, such as animal gnawing, soil movement, or plant root etching, while human butchery likely caused 13 of the marks. Human-caused marks included parallel lines that showed the animal had been cut with a sharp tool or that humans had stripped meat from the bones. She also noted the presence of cut marks on footbones (calcaneus), which might indicate foot removal. Finally, she noted that a single slice mark on a rib may also indicate meat stripping.

Based on these results, Krasinski notes that Lindsay was one of two sites among the eight examined in her study that "demonstrated clear evidence of [human] mammoth utilization in the form of cut marks and fracture patterns." Interestingly, her study showed no evidence of human-caused butchery marks on the bones found at Bluefish Caves, which many archaeologists believed to be a pre-Clovis site. Krasinski further states that it is possible that humans used the sandstone blocks found in association with

Kathryn Krasinski examined the bones of the mammoth uncovered in Lindsay and found these marks, which may have resulted from human butchering. These findings support the idea that humans scavenged the mammoth after it died of natural causes. Courtesy of Museum of the Rockies, Bozeman.

the Lindsay mammoth to break open the animal's large leg bones for marrow extraction. As with more recent Native American cultures, perhaps the earliest people in Montana collected bone marrow and mixed it with meat and berries to make pemmican, a dried, preserved meat product similar to jerky that many Native nations in the region still consider a staple.

If we accept Krasinski's analysis, Lindsay Mammoth—dated to more than twelve thousand years ago—would be the oldest archaeological site in Montana by more than one thousand years. Because of her findings, several archaeologists have included the site as one of the important pre-Clovis sites in North America. For example, Michael Waters and Thomas Stafford, two of the preeminent archaeologists that study early people in North America, include Lindsay in their list of potentially legitimate pre-Clovis sites. They summarize Krasinski's bone analysis data and suggest that it is likely legitimate evidence of people at the site. However, they don't state that the evidence is unequivocal, just that we should consider it as a site that provides evidence of early occupation despite not containing any stone tools. Another important study by Lorena Becerra-Valdiva and Thomas Higham in the journal *Nature* cites Lindsay as one of a handful of sites that show that people were in North America just after the end of the Last Glacial Maximum.

Other scholars, however, do not list the Lindsay Mammoth site as one of the legitimate pre-Clovis sites. For example, in her 2020 *Nature* summary of key pre-Clovis sites, Ruth Gruhn includes many of the sites discussed in this book so far—Manis, Paisley Caves, Cooper's Ferry, and Gault, for example—but does not include Lindsay Mammoth. In a 2017 *Science* article, Todd Braje and colleagues also omit Lindsay from their list of legitimate pre-Clovis sites.

The similarities between the Lindsay Mammoth site and the Schaefer and Hebior sites are tantalizing. Might they collectively suggest a widespread pattern of pre-Clovis mammoth predation by the earliest hunter-gatherers along the edges of the melting Laurentide glacier between 12,300 and 12,500 years ago? Unfortunately, unlike the Wisconsin sites, the excavation of the Lindsay Mammoth failed to yield stone tools. Even just a couple of flaked stone tools used by the hunter-gatherers to butcher the animals would have been enough for most archaeologists to attest to the legitimacy of the sites. For example, in *Strangers in a New Land*, his 2016 book on early sites in the Americas, James Adovasio includes abundant information about Schaefer and Hebior but nothing about the Lindsay site. In *Origin*, her 2022 book on the peopling of the Americas, Jennifer Raff also excludes Lindsay Mammoth from her list of early sites but includes Schaefer and Hebior.

Each of the three sites lack definitive evidence of human predation and instead appear to indicate instances of scavenging. But while the evidence for human butchery is quite convincing at Schaefer and Hebior, it remains rather scant at Lindsay. It might be interesting for an archaeologist to compare the human butchery marks on the elephant bones found at the two pre-Clovis sites in Wisconsin to those found at the Lindsay site, which has a more dubious human association. Perhaps such research could show similarities or differences in the cut marks that may lead to more concrete evidence of the presence or absence of humans at Lindsay.

Until researchers can provide additional evidence of human activity at the site, Lindsay Mammoth will likely not be cited as definitive proof that Native Americans lived in Montana more than twelve thousand years ago. For now, the archaeological data in support of Lindsay appear equivocal, meaning that most experts still doubt about the human presence at the site. There is, however, enough information to suggest that more work needs to be done at the site, through additional excavations, additional analysis of the existing collections at the Museum of the Rockies, and comparison with other sites.

In contrast, archaeological results at all the other sites discussed so far in this book have either contained stone tools or other convincing evidence of human predation or presence. While some archaeologists still debate some of the finer details of these pre-Clovis sites, as discussed earlier in this book, I am convinced that they provide legitimate evidence that people were in North America before Clovis. The twelve-thousand-year-old Manis mastodon in Washington State, for example, was killed using a bone projectile point, but no stone tools were found at the site either. Initially, the Paisley Caves site in Oregon, dating to over twelve thousand years ago, was identified as a pre-Clovis site by the presence of human coprolites (feces), though it too lacked stone tools. These examples suggest that there are additional pre-Clovis sites in North America that may not contain stone tools.

The simplest explanation is that the mammoth found at Lindsay died a natural death and was subjected to animal predation. While the Lindsay Mammoth site may be evidence of the first people in the state of Montana, additional research is necessary to prove it without a doubt. Until then, the Anzick site—the topic of our next chapter—remains the oldest Montana site in the eyes of the broader archaeological community. It is nonetheless exciting to imagine that people were in Montana one thousand years earlier than Anzick.

CHAPTER EIGHT

Montana's Most Important Archaeological Site

Leading experts consider the Anzick site to be the oldest archaeological site in Montana. Archaeologists dispute neither the presence of people at Anzick nor the many radiocarbon dates that show the site to be eleven thousand years old. In addition to being the oldest, Anzick is the state's most important archaeological site. As discussed in chapter 3, its preeminent status stems from the discovery of the only known human skeletal remains at any Clovis site. While dozens of other Clovis sites have been found throughout North America, only Anzick has included human remains.

While archaeologists have identified human skeletal remains that date to about the same time as those found at Anzick at other North American sites, none of these findings have yielded evidence of Clovis culture. The Arlington Springs site in the Channel Islands of California contained human remains dating to more than eleven thousand years ago. In an underwater cavern near the Mexican town of Tulúm, archaeologists recovered the skeletal remains of a woman (nicknamed Eva de Naharron) who lived around the same time as Clovis. Arlington Springs showed a maritime culture due to its location in the Channel Islands, while no associated artifacts were found in the underwater cavern in Mexico. As such, these two very early sets of skeletal remains likely represent cultures that lived in the Americas before Clovis people arrived on the continent. The human remains at Anzick, then, matter to scientists not just due to their antiquity but also because of what they can learn about Clovis burial customs and genetics. Significantly, genetic testing linked the Anzick boy with ancestral human remains in Beringia and descendant remains across North and South America.

Clovis Culture

Clovis artifacts have been found in all forty-eight continental United States, every Canadian province, and in Mexico; it is fitting to call Clovis America's original culture. Archaeologists are not certain whether Clovis technology spread across existing populations via cultural diffusion—for instance, social contact and trade—or whether Clovis people themselves traveled and settled across the continent, potentially mixing with or replacing existing populations. Regardless of how Clovis technology spread, archaeological sites associated with the Clovis culture all date from approximately 11,500 to about 10,800 years ago, give or take a few hundred years.

Archaeologists consider Clovis people the first Native Americans to have lived in Montana. Even the archaeological remains from the Wally's Beach site—just across the Montana state line in Alberta—provide evidence that Clovis people hunted at that site more than 11,400 years ago. If the site's estimated age is accurate, it may indicate that the Clovis culture originated on the northwestern Great Plains, just south of the location where the Ice-Free Corridor emptied into the region. As previously discussed, another Clovis site of roughly the same age, if not a bit earlier, in northern Mexico—El Fin del Mundo—also shows the presence of Clovis hunters. Clovis hunters focused on megafauna that were present across North America. At Wally's Beach, Clovis hunters targeted horses and camels, as well as bison, musk oxen, and caribou, among other large game. At El Fin del Mundo, Clovis hunters targeted gomphotheres, a species of small elephant that went extinct in the region soon after the time of Clovis.

Numerous other Clovis sites exist throughout the western United States, Mexico, and Canada that indicate a heavy reliance on now-extinct megafauna. Montana archaeologist Ruthann Knudson spent her life compiling data from dozens of Clovis and other Paleoindian sites in Montana. Her research was instrumental in establishing that Montana was a hotbed of Clovis activity, even though few Clovis sites have been excavated in the state.

In Wyoming, George Frison's excavations at the Colby Mammoth site yielded the remains of seven mammoths as well as portions of a horse and a camel killed by Clovis hunters about 10,800 years ago. The site also contained evidence of camel predation similar to what researchers found at Wally's Beach in Alberta. At the Mahaffey Clovis site in Boulder, Colorado, protein residue on knives and projectile points indicate the hunting of horses and camels. Several Clovis sites in Arizona, Texas, and New Mexico—including Naco, Gault, and Blackwater Draw, respectively—contain the bones of mammoths and bison, showing that these people relied on large megafauna for subsistence.

Clovis sites are abundant in the eastern United States and appear to be youngest in the far northeast. For example, Maine (Vail) and Nova Scotia (Debert) have two of the most recent Clovis sites anywhere in North America at around 10,600 years ago or so. Of course, Clovis is present in the mid-Atlantic and southeastern United States as well, with sites dating to as early as 11,000 years ago in Pennsylvania (Meadowcroft), Virginia (Cactus Hill), the Carolinas (Topper), and Florida (Little Salt Spring). Each of these sites indicates that people lived in the eastern United States during Clovis. These eastern sites indicate potential pre-Clovis human occupation as well.

Clovis people not only targeted large mammals but also took advantage of all types of foods—plants and animals—available to them. For example, archaeologists at the Gault site in Texas have convincingly shown that Clovis people ate more turtle than they did mammoth. So, while I have characterized Clovis people as driven by the hunting of megafauna, it is also becoming clear that they hunted and gathered a variety of foods across the various habitats in which they lived in North America.

How do archaeologists determine if a site is associated with Clovis culture? First, they consider the age of the site. If a site dates to around eleven thousand years ago, it is likely Clovis. But remember that sites in the far

Clovis hunters used bone, antler, and ivory technology, such as these artifacts from the Anzick site, to hunt and gather in Montana more than eleven thousand years ago. Stocky White photograph

west—California, Utah, Oregon, Idaho, and Washington, among other nearby states—show evidence for the use of Western Stemmed projectile points even earlier than Clovis. So, the age of a given site does not necessarily reveal the culture that inhabited it. Rather, archaeologists usually look for Clovis points. These are very large lanceolate-shaped projectile points that show excellent stone tool manufacture. In fact, archaeologists consider Clovis points to be among the finest projectile points ever produced by humans on earth. This should be expected given the fact that people were hunting mammoths, horses, bison, and camels with them. They needed a superior technology to support their way of life.

Clovis points have very fine bifacial flaking, as well as a characteristic basal-thinning flake, often referred to as a flute-flake, removed from the base. This flute is the most diagnostic attribute of Clovis points. Only its descendent culture—Folsom—has similar flutes; no other cultures in North America produced these styles of fluted projectile points, thus making them unique to Clovis and Folsom.

Along with the fluted points, Clovis sites also yield large blades, scraping tools, and osseous—meaning derived from bone—tools. The osseous tools show a strong reliance on bone, antler, and ivory in tool production, and are likely a descendent technology from the first people on the landscape. These earliest migrants to Montana may not have known where to locate stone sources. It perhaps took a generation or two at least for them to learn the locations of geological seams of toolstone. Remember, the very first people to places like Montana would have had to learn the landscape and figure out where to find good quality stone to make their points. Until that time, they likely relied on a range of more readily available materials, including bone, antler, ivory, and wood.

One of the interesting things about the Anzick site is the presence of osseous tools similar to those found at much earlier sites in what used to be Beringia. For example, the bone rods from Anzick closely resemble those from the Upward Sun River, Broken Mammoth, and Holzman sites in Alaska, as well as some found at the Yana Rhinoceros Horn site in Siberia. These similarities are not coincidental. As with the genetics of the people that lived at Anzick, their cultures and tool types are also derivative of their progenitors in Beringia during the Last Glacial Maximum.

One of the other hallmark traits of Clovis sites is their reliance on high-quality sources of stone to make their tools. As discussed above, this implies that Clovis people had learned their landscape well enough that they had found the important geological outcrops of toolstone. This certainly implies that the earlier ancestors of Clovis people were present in the region for at least a couple of generations prior to adopting what we've described as Clovis culture, including their diagnostic projectile points. Does this mean that locations like the Lindsay Mammoth site provide evidence of that earlier human presence? Possibly. Or, it means that there are other unidentified archaeological sites that we simply have not found yet.

Archaeology of the Anzick Site

Samuel "Stocky" White—one of my former students at the University of Montana—completed his dissertation on the Anzick site in 2019. White spent much of his youth in the town of Livingston, Montana, about thirty miles south of the Anzick site. In Livingston, White had the good fortune to learn about archaeology from local professionals such as Dr. Larry Lahren, whose book *Homeland* contains excellent information on the finds at Anzick and other local Livingston-area archaeological sites. Using information from Lahren and other researchers, White pieced together the existing information about the Anzick site. His dissertation was the first attempt to compile everything that archaeologists know about Anzick, from its discovery to current efforts to interpret the site.

The Anzick site was discovered in 1961 when local resident Bill Bray found a very large biface and "some bones covered with red stuff" while he was fishing near the site. Another seven years passed by before local residents Ben Hargis and Calvin Sarver found the human skeletal remains and associated stone and bone tools. In 1968, Hargis and Sarver were excavating dirt and rock from the area of the site to use in a septic tank drain field for a parking lot at Wilsall High School, roughly two miles from the site. As White explains in his dissertation, the two witnessed "an unusual powdery material that fell out of the hillside." They also noticed a large biface that fell out of the backhoe bucket. They stopped their work and began to dig with hand tools into the face of the rocky slope. After finishing their work for the day, the two men brought their wives back to the site that evening and conducted more excavations. They found many more stone artifacts covered in "red stuff." They also noted that the artifacts were "tightly stacked" in a small area measuring about a few feet in diameter. The red, powdery material covered the artifacts within a small area in the cliff face.

Toward the bottom of the stack of artifacts, the group collected human bones that were covered with the same red powder. White identified these bones as the "Anzick 1" individual, directly associated with the other Clovis artifacts at the site. A second set of human remains—called "Anzick 2"—were found several meters away and were not associated with the Clovis culture. Instead, that burial dated to approximately eight thousand years ago.

The Crazy Mountains, seen in this 1894 F. Jay Haynes photograph, rise just west of present-day Wilsall, Montana. This landscape would have been familiar to the people living in the region at the same time as the Anzick boy.
H-03163, Montana State Historical Society Photograph Archives

It seems that the area of the Anzick site was a perennial burial ground for Native Americans. Interestingly, the Wilsall cemetery is near the Anzick site as well. As Stocky White writes in his dissertation, perhaps this area has a spiritual pull that has led people to bury their dead there for the past eleven thousand years.

After the two families removed the artifacts from the hillside rockshelter, they took them home and cleaned them off in a sink. As White describes, their goal was to get all of the "red stuff" off the artifacts. We now know that the "red stuff" was red ochre, or hematite, a common mineral found in the Rocky Mountains of Montana. The Native Americans of the region used red ochre to decorate their bodies, clothing, and shelters, and to produce art. It is also commonly found covering human remains at burial sites across the Great Plains and Rocky Mountains. Several of the artifacts from the Anzick site still retain small red ochre stains, but for the most part it was removed during that initial cleaning in 1968.

After discovering the site, Hargis and Sarver notified Larry Lahren, then a graduate student at the University of Montana in Missoula. Lahren's examination of the collection resulted in the Anzick site being officially recorded by the Montana State Historic Preservation Office (SHPO) as site 24PA506. This means that the Anzick site is the 506th site found in Park (PA) County within the state of Montana, which is twenty-fourth alphabetically of the fifty US states. Lahren contacted Professor Dee Taylor at the University of Montana, who determined that the site was so destroyed that additional archaeology would not be able to determine its true age. Despite this initial assumption, subsequent research by Lahren and White, among others, shows that the Anzick site assemblage is associated with the Clovis culture, including the stone tools and the Anzick 1 human remains. They found several Clovis-style fluted projectile points, bifaces, and bone rods similar to those found at other Clovis sites across North America.

The Anzick Artifact Assemblage

The Anzick stone tool assemblage includes seventy-two bifaces, seven unifaces, eight projectile points (or point preforms), fourteen stone tool fragments, and fifteen osseous tools. In the 1990s, archaeologists Julie Morrow and Stuart Fiedel identified the osseous tools as likely being produced from elk antler. In addition to the stone and bone tools, the Clovis-age human remains include part of a skull, a clavicle (shoulder bone), and a rib fragment. The rest of the skeletal remains likely vanished over time due to natural processes, such as animal scavenging, flooding, and erosion from the nearby creek.

The Anzick boy was buried with more than one hundred artifacts, including these beautiful examples of Clovis bifaces and other stone tools. Stocky White photograph

Many archaeologists, myself included, interpret the entire Clovis assemblage at Anzick to be offerings of tools by multiple family members in honor of the deceased, now known to be the remains of a two-year-old boy. After the young boy passed away it would seem his family honored his burial with tools that he might be able to use in the afterlife. The red ochre covered the remains of the tools and the boy as a ceremonial offering, as with many burials across Montana for the subsequent eleven thousand years. Even burials in ancestral Beringia—including Upward Sun River and Mal'ta—contained evidence of red ochre.

The Anzick burial was likely quite emotional for the boy's family. Given the very low populations of Clovis people at that time, the loss of any individual was a significant event for a small family group. The hunter-gatherers at Anzick valued the tools interred with the two-year-old boy; they could have used them to hunt and butcher mammoths, horses, and camels. Instead, they left them in the grave of their deceased family member.

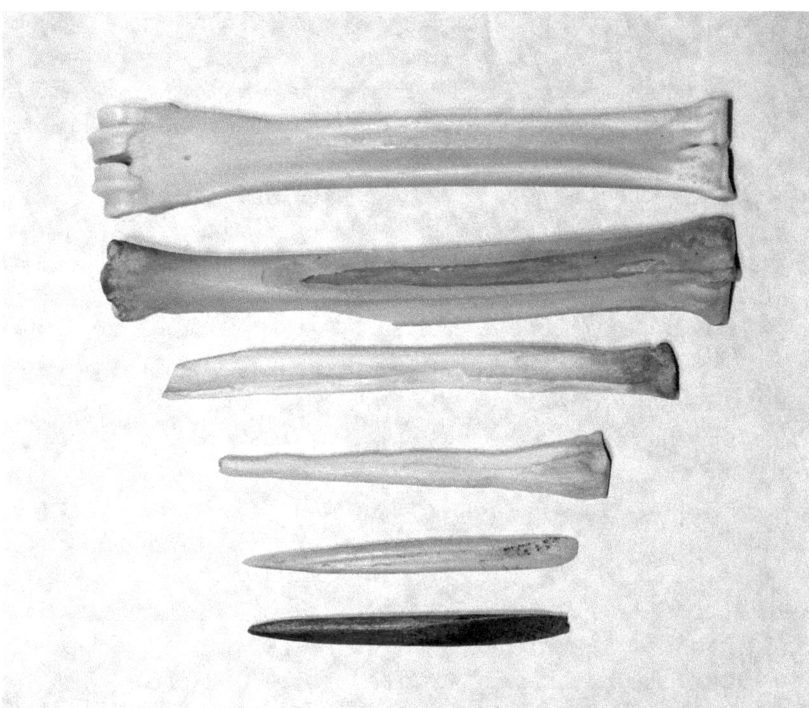

Stocky White re-created the bone rods from the Anzick site in hopes of determining how Clovis people produced and used them eleven thousand years ago.
Stocky White photograph

Given the Clovis age of the human remains and associated artifacts, the Anzick site has been the subject of intensive analysis and dating. Numerous radiocarbon dates have been assayed for the organic materials at the site, including the human remains and bone rods. Most of the initial dates from the 1980s placed the items at around 10,600 to 10,900 years old. More recently, modern radiocarbon methodologies have led to more accurate dating of the Anzick remains and bone artifacts. In their 2006 study of the artifacts, Julie Morrow and Stuart Fiedel dated one of the bone tools to 11,040 years ago, as well as a portion of the human clavicle to about 10,800 years ago. Since those dates, additional radiocarbon dating indicates that the elk antler tools, as well as the human remains, date to approximately 10,900–11,000 years ago. This makes it the oldest well-dated site in Montana that can be irrefutably linked to Native American hunter-gatherers. While the Lindsay Mammoth site is more than 1,000 years older, the human association with that location remains in doubt. Until that question is resolved, the Anzick site remains Montana's oldest archaeological site.

The associated stone and bone tools from Anzick typify those found at other Clovis sites throughout the western United States, Mexico, and Canada. The tools include a variety of bifaces in all stages of manufacture, produced from at least five different high-quality stone sources throughout the Rocky Mountains and Great Plains, and some finished projectile points. Clovis hunters likely used the elk antler rods as foreshafts in atlatls (tools used to throw spears), although their precise function has been a matter of debate. Some suggest that they might actually be projectile points, perhaps similar to the mastodon bone point used to kill the mastodon found at Manis in Washington.

Archaeologists have noted similar stone and bone tools at many other western Clovis sites, including the Richey-Roberts site in Washington; the Simon Cache in Idaho; the Fenn Cache in the Utah, Wyoming, and Idaho borderlands; the Mahaffey Cache in Colorado; and the Hogeye Clovis cache in Texas, among other sites in the western United States. Many of these sites have similar assemblages of artifacts and may represent human burials as well; however, to date, only the Anzick site has yielded evidence of human remains associated with the Clovis assemblage of artifacts. Archaeologists have interpreted the other sites, for now, to be caches, perhaps tool storage for mobile hunter-gatherers to collect for use later.

One of the most important contributions of Stocky White's dissertation research is the protein residue analysis that he conducted on several of the Anzick artifacts. White transported several of the tools to the PaleoResearch lab operated by Linda Scott Cummings in Colorado. Although humans had handled the artifacts for years, three of the six artifacts submitted for protein residue analysis yielded positive results, with one pointing to a now-extinct camel and another testing positive for rabbit. Like Wally's Beach in Alberta, Mahaffey in Colorado, and Colby in Wyoming, Anzick is one of only four Clovis sites to yield evidence of camel predation.

Another incredible discovery from White's research was that hunters used a handful of the larger bifaces to shape the bone rods found at Anzick. White conducted experiments in which he replicated the production techniques that Clovis people used to make the bone rods. He was able to show not only how the bone rods were made but also that they fit within the notches in several of the large bifaces from the site. Clovis people used a variety of bone, antler, and ivory materials to produce the rods. Once they were in their desired shape and size, Clovis people then used the notches on the bifaces to conduct the final shaping of the osseous rods.

At eleven thousand years old, the Anzick site is Montana's oldest Clovis site and the only one in the world with Clovis human remains. As described earlier, the genetic analysis of the Anzick boy's remains by Eske Willerslev and his colleagues reveals the child to be an ancestor of the people that lived in Beringia during the Last Glacial Maximum, more than

Stocky White's analysis showed that Clovis people shaped the bone rods found at the Anzick site by using the notches in large stone bifaces, as shown in this photograph.
Stocky White photograph

fifteen thousand years ago. Genetics also show that the boy's relatives and their descendants spread throughout North and South America to become the hundreds of Indigenous cultures of the Americas. The Anzick boy and associated burial goods are truly remarkable finds, significant not just for Montana history but for understanding the origins of Native American cultures across the Americas.

In 2014, the skeletal remains of the two-year-old boy from Anzick, as well as those from the eight-thousand-year-old Anzick-2 skeleton—were reburied by the Anzick family in a proper ceremony conducted with local Native American tribes. Archaeologists and geneticists were also present to memorialize the reburial of the most important skeleton in Montana history. While the human remains are no longer available for scientific analysis, their reburial marked an emotional conclusion to a remarkable chapter of Montana's Native American history. The study of the Anzick remains brought archaeologists, geneticists, and tribal members together in pursuit of the important goal of understanding human origins, ensuring that future generations would understand the past in a dynamic way.

✷

CHAPTER NINE

Where to Go from Here?

Montana's first people were Native American hunter-gatherers who made a great journey spanning thousands of years. Starting in Eurasia thirty thousand years ago, people spread northward into Siberia, both through the interior of the region as well as along the coast. In Beringia, at least twenty thousand years ago, interior and coastal hunter-gatherers moved into the region to become the ancestral Beringian population—the ultimate source of all Native American cultures. Sometime around fifteen thousand to twenty thousand years ago, a portion of that early Beringian population traveled down the Pacific Coast into North and South America. If the human footprints in White Sands National Park, New Mexico, in fact date to twenty-three thousand years ago, people must have initiated that travel even earlier.

Regardless, people eventually arrived in North America and settled in places like the northwest coast of North America. Archaeological sites in Oregon, Washington, California, Texas, Wisconsin, Idaho, and elsewhere show people living throughout the United States by roughly twelve thousand to thirteen thousand years ago. The Lindsay Mammoth site may indicate the presence of people in Montana by then as well. Certainly, by the time of Clovis, we know that people had arrived in Montana, as evidenced by the Wally's Beach and Anzick sites.

But while some of the earliest sites in North America are found in the far western portions of North America, including Alaska, Oregon, and Washington, the same people who migrated through the interior rivers from the coast may not have been the first to settle in Montana. Thirteen thousand years ago, people also started to migrate south from Alaska (eastern Beringia) through the Ice-Free Corridor. These people moved along the Rocky Mountain Front through the Canadian provinces to arrive in Montana by

Indigenous people moving south through the Ice-Free Corridor likely traversed the eastern edge of the Rocky Mountain Front. Along the way, they would have encountered natural features such as the Chinese Wall in north-central Montana, seen here in an August 1965 photograph taken by C. H. McDonald.

U.S. Forest Service photo 513802, Bud Moore Papers, 1805–2011, MSS 848, Archives and Special Collections, Mansfield Library, University of Montana

the time we start to see people—either 12,300 years ago at Lindsay Mammoth or 11,400 years ago at Wally's Beach in Alberta.

Much archaeological work still needs to be done to resolve two major issues concerning early Native American history and archaeology in Montana: Which route (or routes) did the first Montanans take to get to Montana, and when did they first arrive? I hope the reader is not frustrated by the fact that I don't have the definitive answers to these questions. But let me explain.

First, archaeologists have abundant data that could be used to support either a coastal migration route (see chapter 5) or a migration through the Ice-Free Corridor (see chapter 6). The earliest Native Americans to arrive in Montana could have traveled down the Pacific Coast and then inland via river valleys, including the Columbia, Snake, and Clark Fork. Alternatively, they could have traveled down the Ice-Free Corridor that opened thirteen thousand years ago and still arrived in Montana by the time archaeologists have estimated that people first lived in the region, around twelve thousand years ago or so. In the end, I think it is likely that Native Americans traveled both routes and that archaeologists will eventually find evidence that the first Montanans used both the Ice-Free Corridor and the coastal route.

Of course, Native Americans know their history and have used oral narratives to document it over millennia, as discussed in chapter 1. These histories offer context for the lives of their ancestors, provide guidance, and convey moral and ethical values. While their oral histories, passed down from generation to generation over millennia, are significant on their own, researchers can learn a great deal from them. Native American histories, such as those tribal elders recounted to anthropologists like James Teit, Franz Boas, and Clark Wissler, and the origin stories they continue to tell, can enhance understandings of archaeological data and help researchers pursue new information that might better explain the origins of the first Montanans.

In addition to ethnohistories, archaeologists should continue to look for evidence of the first Montanans in ancient river valleys that might have been used by the first people as travel corridors both in western Montana, to support the Pacific Coast route, and north-central Montana, to support the Ice-Free Corridor route. In western Montana, the Clark Fork and Salmon River valleys, as well as the region of Lolo and Lookout Passes might be good places to look. In north-central Montana, the region of the Blackfeet Indian Reservation as well as the Missouri River valley and those of its larger tributaries, including the Milk and Sun Rivers, likely have very old sites that date to the time of the first people.

From the outset, this book established that the first people in Montana were hunter-gatherers who traveled long distances from northeast Asia, Alaska, and Canada to get to Montana. The last few chapters have clarified a few more aspects of this history. Archaeologists know, for instance, that the first Montanans arrived here sometime around twelve thousand years ago, though people had settled in other places in North and South America much earlier than that. Of course, some archaeologists contend that sites like Paisley Caves in Oregon and Manis Mastodon in Washington aren't representative of the first peoples. This despite the fact that Paisley Caves contains human feces dated to more than twelve thousand years ago, while Manis Mastodon yielded human tools used around that time as well.

The archaeological and ethnohistorical data suggest that the first Americans used both the Ice-Free Corridor and coastal routes, but they perhaps took the coastal route earlier (though not necessarily to get to Montana). The earliest sites show a reliance on maritime as well as inland resources. If people indeed arrived in New Mexico by twenty-three thousand years ago, it looks like they also stalked and hunted giant sloth. These people adapted to the world around them, hunting, gathering, and fishing across a wide variety of habitats.

Certainly, these people may have experienced hardship, including starvation, times when natural remedies could not heal a wound, and perhaps a death twenty to thirty years earlier than most Americans might expect today. Hunter-gatherers who lived to the age of fifty or so were elders; today, that is considered middle age. We are lucky to have modern technology to help us survive illness and injury. Despite such modern advances, our contemporary world continues to develop technology to slowly and gradually destroy the environment, including its plants, animals, and people.

Such concepts would be extremely difficult to explain to a time-traveling hunter-gatherer. Would a Clovis hunter understand our way of life, or why we developed technologies to become wealthier at the expense of our neighbors, or ones that create pollution, degrade the environment, increase solar radiation, and dry the water sources essential to human survival? Sharing resources is a hallmark trait of nearly all hunter-gatherer societies. They facilitated these practices through widespread kinship and family networks that allowed for human survival in the face of occasional resource stress. Human networks were the key to survival, not wealth. Many if not most hunter-gatherers scorned wealth and the accumulation of goods. How could a hunter-gatherer be expected to move from place to place on an almost daily basis while carrying large amounts of stuff that wasn't essential to their survival? The entire toolkit of a Clovis hunter, like those that lived at the Anzick site in Montana eleven thousand years ago, could probably fit in a leather satchel or a backpack. Additional equipment—perhaps stone material, foodstuffs, and leather hides for a lodge covering—were likely attached to a dog travois for transport.

Today, many people seek to accumulate wealth, often at the expense of others. If a hunter-gatherer undertook such an effort, that person would have been explicitly ridiculed and shamed in their society. It would not have been feasible or acceptable to hoard wealth when someone else was hungry. The hunter-gatherer lifestyle did not accept people who didn't share available resources.

To consider the origins of the first Indigenous people to arrive in Montana is really to ask a question about humanity and the ancestry of all people. To understand the first Montanans is to understand hunter-gatherers across the world and the behaviors that allowed us to be successful everywhere we traveled, whether it was Asia, Australia, Africa, Europe, Polynesia, or the Americas.

While there are still some people who live in remote areas of our planet—such as the Amazon River valley of Brazil, where groups of people still live as hunter-gatherers—for the most part, that lifestyle is extinct.

Rollin H. McKay photographed these flowering bitterroots in 1940. The official state flower of Montana, these plants, known for their vibrant pink color, are increasingly difficult to find in the wild, and state and federal laws prevent foragers from harvesting them. 94.3118, Archives and Special Collections, Mansfield Library, University of Montana

There may not be any hunter-gatherers today that haven't had contact with the modern world in some shape or form. While many people in Montana and elsewhere hunt and gather berries, they do so in places where their various governments allow them to do so. For instance, if I wanted to collect bitterroot in my hometown of Missoula, Montana, where it used to be plentiful, I would have to grow it myself in a greenhouse—it would be illegal for me to collect natural specimens. It is rare to find native bitterroot on the natural landscape anymore. When I come across fields of bitterroot in my journeys to places like Yellowstone's foothills, I am always pleasantly surprised that such an amazing natural resource has survived in the face of modern development.

It is no longer feasible to be a hunter-gatherer in our world. Private property laws prevent public access to large swaths of land, while many federal laws limit human activities on public land, making it illegal to collect many edible plants and hunt animals in the numbers that would be needed to allow a hunter-gatherer population to survive in today's world.

I doubt that Montana's first peoples would have believed this place could change so dramatically. Sure, the earliest Montanans saw environmental changes decimate mammoths, mastodons, sloths, horses, and camels. But they survived by adapting to the changing landscape. They quickly realized that they needed to hunt bison, marmot, and rabbit and collect pine nuts and bitterroot, which their descendants continued to do for thousands of years until Lewis and Clark arrived in 1805.

I look forward to the next fifty years of archaeology in Montana. I hope that we find archaeological sites that help us understand more precisely the chronology of the first Montanans, as well as the travel routes they took to get here. I expect that someone will revisit the Lindsay Mammoth site and resolve the question as to its human association. I expect the discovery of other ancient archaeological sites will help us better answer the questions posed in this book. I hope that this quest will also force people to come to grips with the daunting task of modern environmental change. Perhaps we can look back to Montana's first peoples and their thousands of years of hunter-gatherer survival in this land of beginnings to help us learn how to sustainably meet the challenges of the modern world.

✷

GLOSSARY

archaeological survey. The process by which archaeologists find sites in a landscape; it often involves walking, or pedestrian survey, and shovel test pit excavation.

atlatl. Throwing spear and handle used by hunter-gatherers in Montana from 11,000 to 1,500 years ago; it was replaced by the bow and arrow.

Beringia. A large landmass that existed in Alaska and Siberia in the area that is now the Bering Strait between the Arctic and Pacific Oceans. The landmass ceased to exist when glaciers melted at the end of the ice age between 15,000 and 12,000 years ago.

biface (bifacial). A tool produced by removing flakes from two sides of a stone to produce a sharp projectile point or knife.

bifurcate. A projectile point or knife with an indented (concave) base.

bone rods. Tools made of bone and used by Clovis people in Montana. These rods may have been the foreshafts of atlatls.

cache. A location where a large group of tools was left with the expectation of future use. Clovis people in the Great Plains regularly stored tools in this manner.

chert. A stone material made mostly of cryptocrystalline quartz, making it conducive to sharp edges. In Montana, it most commonly forms in limestone.

Clovis. One of the earliest cultures in the Americas (around 11,000 years ago), named after Clovis, New Mexico, where it was first identified.

coprolite. Waste from a biological organism.

Cordilleran glacier. A large ice sheet that covered millions of miles along the Pacific Coast of North America about 2.6 million years ago.

debitage. The debris generated during the manufacture of a stone tool.

Denali Complex. A human culture that lived in Beringia and Alaska during the Late Pleistocene. The same people and customs are known as the Dyuktai Culture (Siberia) and Paleoarctic tradition.

DNA. A self-replicating material contained in the chromosomes of all living organisms. It is the carrier of genetic information that can be compared between individuals to track human migration across the world.

Dyuktai Culture. A human culture that existed in Beringia and Siberia during the Late Pleistocene, also known as the Denali Complex or the Paleoarctic Tradition, as they are called in Alaska.

ethnoarchaeology. The study of modern people and their ways of life in hopes of better understanding and interpreting ancient archaeological sites.

faunal remains. The remains of animals found at archaeological and paleontological sites.

flaking. The process of removal of debitage during stone tool manufacture; a synonym of flintknapping.

flintknapping. Stone tool manufacture (see also flaking).

fluted. A projectile point with a flake removed from the center of the base parallel to its lateral margins. This feature is unique to the Clovis and Folsom cultures of the Great Plains and Rocky Mountains.

Folsom. A Paleoindian culture of the Great Plains that existed between 10,900 and 10,200 years ago.

Folsom point. A form of projectile point used during the Folsom period. These points are commonly fluted, although unfluted varieties were used as well.

foreshaft. Part of an atlatl; the projectile point was hafted to the foreshaft, and the foreshaft fit into the main dart shaft.

genetic research. The study of DNA to learn about biological organisms. Archaeologists of early people in the Americas primarily use genetic research to trace human and other biological organisms' movements across landscapes.

Glacial Lake Missoula. A vast glacial lake that existed during the Late Pleistocene in the vicinity of what is today Missoula, Montana. As glaciers melted roughly 15,000 years ago, the lake emptied across northwestern Montana into eastern Washington and Oregon.

Goshen. A Paleoindian culture of the northern Great Plains that existed just after Clovis and Folsom. Goshen projectile points were not fluted, however.

grinding stone. A large rock with a flat surface upon which to prepare foods, including seeds, berries, roots, and meat.

haplogroup. A combination of genes at different chromosomal regions that are closely linked and that tend to be inherited together. Groups of similar organisms will be part of the same haplogroup.

hearth. A fire pit. It is the most common feature found at archaeology sites in Montana and was used for cooking food or providing heat.

Holocene. The modern geological epoch, which began following the Pleistocene, roughly 11,000 years ago.

hunter-gatherer. A person who makes a living by hunting and gathering their food.

Ice-Free Corridor. The inland corridor that opened between the Laurentide and Cordilleran Ice Sheets around 13,000 to 12,000 years ago between Alaska and Montana.

interstadial. A warming period during an ice age.

kill site. A location where a hunter-gatherer killed and butchered an animal for food.

lanceolate point. A lance-shaped projectile point common to the Paleoindian period from 11,000 to 8,000 years ago. They are long, wide, and thin with straight or concave bases and gently tapering lateral margins. Clovis, Goshen, and Folsom points are types of lanceolate points.

Last Glacial Maximum (LGM). The peak period of cold and ice during the Late Pleistocene, between about 25,000 and 18,000 years ago.

Laurentide glacier. A massive ice sheet that covered millions of miles, including much of North America, between about 2.6 million years ago to the present.

marrow. A fatty substance within animal bones that provided a significant source of food for hunter-gatherers across the world.

megafauna. Large animals common to the Pleistocene geologic epoch. Many species of megafauna became extinct in North America about 11,000 years ago or so. Today, elephants in Africa are an example of megafauna.

microblade. A thin and long stone tool produced from flintknapping a wedge-shaped core as part of the Dyuktai, Denali, or Paleoarctic traditions of Beringia. Hunters inserted microblades into bone point tips to kill animals.

obsidian. A high-quality volcanic glass used throughout the world for stone tool manufacture. It is the sharpest natural material known to humans.

occupation. A specific period when people lived at an archaeological site. Sites often feature multiple occupations.

ochre. A soft iron oxide mineral used by Native Americans in Montana as a pigment. It is usually red, but sometimes produces other colors, and commonly used in rock art. Archaeologists have found it coating artifacts, and the material is associated with burials.

Pacific Coast route. The likely route that the first people took from Beringia down the west coast of North America to first migrate to North and South America during the Late Pleistocene.

Paleoindian. Any variety of North American human culture that existed prior to 9,000 or so years ago.

paleontological site. A site that contains a deceased ancient animal or other biological organism typically not associated with humans.

pithouse. A subterranean or semi-subterranean structure used by hunter-gatherers across the world. They had a portion of the house belowground, with the remainder covered by a wooden or other type of structure.

Pleistocene. The geologic epoch that spanned between 2 million and 11,000 years ago.

pre-Clovis. Any human culture that existed in the Americas before Clovis, approximately 11,000 years ago or so.

preform. A stone tool in its early stages of manufacture.

pressure flaker. A handheld bone, wood, or antler tool used to remove small pieces of debitage in the final steps of stone tool manufacture.

processing site. Location where hunter-gatherers processed a resource (stone, animal, or plant) in preparation for later consumption or use.

projectile. A thrown object. In Montana, projectiles were usually spear or arrow points made of stone and used to kill animals for food.

quarry. Location where hunter-gatherers obtained stone for making tools.

quartzite. A metamorphic rock composed of quartz sandstone; often used in stone tool manufacture in Montana.

radiocarbon. The radioactive isotope of carbon. It decays at a fixed rate that can be measured to determine the date of an organism's death.

radiocarbon calibrations. A process by which radiocarbon dates are adjusted so they read in a standard calendar system; calibrations are typically completed by analysis of tree rings or ice cores.

radiocarbon date. A chronometric dating method of organic material in which archaeologists determine the age of an archaeological site, artifact, or feature, with an accuracy of between thirty and fifty years on average.

scraper. Stone tool used to scrape hides for preparation as clothing. Scrapers may be handheld or hafted onto handles.

Solutrean. A prehistoric culture that existed in Europe approximately 21,000 to 18,000 years ago.

stratigraphy. The order and position of layers of soils, artifacts, and materials at archaeological sites. Older layers are deeper (near the bottom) in the stratigraphy than more recent layers (near the top).

subsistence. Making a living by hunting, gathering, fishing, or agriculture.

unifacial. A stone tool with debitage removed from only one side, usually to form a cutting or scraping edge.

Western Stemmed projectile points. A type of projectile point used during the Late Pleistocene across western North America and in some areas of the Pacific Rim.

BIBLIOGRAPHY

Ackerman, Robert E. "Cave 1, Lime Hills." In *American Beginnings: The Prehistory and Paleoecology of Beringia*, edited by F. H. West, 470–77. Chicago: University of Chicago Press, 1996.

Adovasio, James M., and David Pedler. *Strangers in a New Land: What Archaeology Reveals about the First Americans*. Richmond, ON: Firefly Books, 2016.

Baumler, Mark F., and Leslie B. Davis. "Upon Closer Examination: Paleoindian Behavioral Inferences from a Folsom Feature Lithic Assemblage at the Indian Creek Occupation Site, West-Central Montana Rockies." *Archaeology in Montana* 41:2 (2000): 17–42.

Beck, Charlotte, and Tom Jones. "Clovis and Western Stemmed: Population Migration and the Meeting of Two Technologies in the Intermountain West." *American Antiquity* 75:1 (2010): 81–116.

Bennett, Matthew R., David Bustos, Jeffrey S. Pigati, Kathleen B. Springer, Thomas M. Urban, Vance T. Holliday, Sally C. Reynolds, Marcin Budka, Jeffrey S. Honke, and Daniel Odess. "Evidence of Humans in North America during the Last Glacial Maximum." *Science* 373:6562 (Sep. 24, 2021): 1528–31.

Bjornstad, Bruce N. *On the Trail of the Ice Age Floods: A Geological Field Guide to the Mid-Columbia Basin*. Sandpoint, ID: Keokee Books, 2006.

Boas, Franz, ed. *Folk Tales of Salishan and Sahaptin Tribes*. Lancaster, PA: American Folklore Society, 1917.

Bourgeon, Lauriane, and Ariane Burke. "Horse Exploitation by Beringian Hunters during the Last Glacial Maximum." *Quaternary Science Reviews* 269 (Oct. 1, 2021): 1–16.

———, Ariane Burke, and Thomas Higham. "Earliest Human Presence in North America Dated to the Last Glacial Maximum: New Radiocarbon Dates from Bluefish Caves, Canada." *PLOS ONE* 12:1 (2017): 1–15.

Cinq-Mars, J. "Bluefish Cave I: A Late Pleistocene Eastern Beringian Cave Deposit in the Northern Yukon." *Canadian Journal of Archaeology* 3 (1979): 1–32.

Clark, Peter U., Arthur S. Dyke, Jeremy D. Shakun, Anders E. Carlson, Jorie Clark, Barbara Wohlfarth, Jerry X. Mitrovica, Steven W. Hostetler, and A. Marshall McCabe. "The Last Glacial Maximum." *Science* 325:5941 (Aug. 7, 2009): 710–14.

Clarkson, Chris, Zenobia Jacobs, Ben Marwick, Richard Fullagar, Lynley Wallis, Mike Smith, and Richard G. Roberts et al . "Human Occupation of Northern Australia by 65,000 Years Ago." *Nature* 547:7663 (Jul. 20, 2017): 306–10.

Davis, Leslie B. "In Search of Early Elephants." *Montana Outdoors*, Nov.–Dec. 1986, 27–31.

———. "Paleo-Indian Archaeology in the High Plains and Rocky Mountains of Montana." In *From Kostenki to Clovis: Upper Paleolithic-Paleo-Indian Adaptations*, edited by Olga Soffer and N. D. Praslov, 263–77. New York: Springer, 1993.

———, Stephen Aaberg, and James Schmitt. *The Obsidian Cliff Plateau Prehistoric Lithic Source, Yellowstone National Park, Wyoming*. Mammoth, WY: Yellowstone National Park Center for Resources, 1995.

———, John P. Albanese, Linda Scott Cummings, and John W. Fisher Jr. "Reappraisal of the MacHaffie Site Paleoindian Occupational Sequence." *Current Research in the Pleistocene* 8 (1991):17–20.

———, and Mark F. Baumler. "Clovis and Folsom Occupations at Indian Creek." *Current Research in the Pleistocene* 17 (2000):17–19.

———, and Sally T. Greiser. "Indian Creek Paleoindians: Early Occupation of the Elkhorn Mountains' Southeast Flank, West-Central Montana." In *Ice Age Hunters of the Rockies*, edited by D. J. Stanford and J. S. Day, 225–83. Denver: Museum of Natural History, Denver, and Niwot: University Press of Colorado.

———, Christopher Hill, and John W. Fisher Jr. "Radiocarbon Dates for Paleoindian Components (Folsom, Scottsbluff) at the MacHaffie Site, West-Central Montana Rockies." *Current Research in the Pleistocene* 19 (2003):18–20.

———, and M. C. Wilson. "The Late Pleistocene Lindsay Mammoth (24DW501), Eastern Montana." *Current Research in the Pleistocene* 2 (1985): 97–98.

Davis, L. G. "Late Upper Paleolithic Occupation at Cooper's Ferry, Idaho, USA, ~16,000 Years Ago." *Science* 365:6456 (Aug. 30, 2019): 891–97.

Dillehay, Thomas D., C. Ramirez, M. Pino, M. B. Collins, J. Rossen, and J. D. Pino-Navarro. "Monte Verde: Seaweed, Food, Medicine, and the Peopling of South America." *Science* 784:5877 (May 9, 2008): 784–86.

Dixon, E. James. *Bones, Boats, and Bison: Archeology and the First Colonization of Western North America*. Albuquerque: University of New Mexico Press, 1999.

Elias, S. A., and J. Brigham-Grette. "Late Pleistocene Glacial Events in Beringia." *Encyclopedia of Quaternary Science* (2013): 191–201.

———, and B. Crocker. "The Bering Land Bridge: A Moisture Barrier to the Dispersal of Steppe-Tundra Biota?" *Quaternary Science Review* 27 (Dec. 2008): 2473–83.

Endacott, N. A. "The Zooarchaeology of Lime Hills Cave: Paleoecological and Taphonomic Insights." PhD dissertation, Washington State University, Pullman, 2008.

Erlandson, Jon M., T. J. Braje, K. M. Gill, and M. H. Graham. "Ecology of the Kelp Highway: Did Marine Resources Facilitate Human Dispersal from Northeast Asia to the Americas?" *Journal of Island and Coastal Archaeology* 10:3 (2015): 392–411.

———, Michael H. Graham, Bruce J. Bourque, Debra Corbett, James A. Estes, and Robert S. Steneck. "The Kelp Highway Hypothesis: Marine Ecology, the Coastal Migration Theory, and the Peopling of the Americas." *Journal of Island and Coastal Archaeology* 2:2 (2007): 161–74.

Fedge, Daryl W., James M. White, Michael C. Wilson, D. Erle Nelson, John S. Vogel, and John R. Southon. "Vermillion Lakes Site: Adaptations and Environments in the Canadian Rockies during the Latest Pleistocene and Early Holocene." *American Antiquity* 60:1 (Jan. 1995): 81–108.

Fiedel, Stuart J. "The Anzick Genome Proves Clovis Is First, After All." *Quaternary International*, Jul. 20, 2017, 4–9.

Firestone, Richard B., A. West, J. P. Kennett, L. Becker, T. E. Bunch, Z. S. Revay, and P. H. Schultz et al. "Evidence for an Extraterrestrial Impact 12,900 Years Ago that Contributed to the Megafaunal Extinctions and the Younger Dryas Cooling." *Proceedings of the National Academy of Sciences* 104:41 (2007): 16016–21.

Fladmark, Knut R., Jonathan C. Driver, and Diana Alexander. "The Paleoindian Component at Charlie Lake Cave (HbRf 39), British Columbia." *American Antiquity* 53:2 (Apr. 1988): 371–84.

Forbis, Richard G. "The MacHaffie Site." PhD dissertation, Columbia University, New York, 1955.

———, and John D. Sperry. "Early Man Site in Montana." *American Antiquity* 18:2 (Oct. 1952): 127–33.

Frison, George C. *The Mill Iron Site*. Albuquerque: University of New Mexico Press, 1996.

———. *Survival by Hunting: Prehistoric Human Predators and Animal Prey*. Berkeley: University of California Press, 2004.

———, and Lawrence C. Todd. *The Colby Mammoth Site: Taphonomy and Archaeology of a Clovis Kill in Northern Wyoming*. Albuquerque: University of New Mexico Press, 1986.

Froese, Duane, Mathias Stiller, Peter D. Heintzman, Alberto V. Reyes, Grant D. Zazula, André E. R. Soares, and Matthias Meyer et al. "Fossil and Genomic Evidence Constrains the Timing of Bison Arrival in North America." *Proceedings of the National Academy of Sciences* 114:13 (2017): 3457–62.

Goebel, T, Sergei B. Slobodin, and Michael R. Waters. "New Dates from Ushki-1, Kamchatka, Confirm 13,000 cal BP Age for Earliest Paleolithic Occupation." *Journal of Archaeological Science* 37:10 (Oct. 2010): 2640–49.

———, M. R. Waters, and D. H. O'Rourke. "The Late Pleistocene Dispersal of Modern Humans in the Americas." *Science* 319:5869 (Mar. 14, 2008): 1497–1502.

Gould, Richard A. *Living Archaeology*. London: Cambridge University Press, 1980.

Graf, Kelly E., and Ian Buvit, "Human Dispersal from Siberia to Beringia: Assessing a Beringian Standstill in Light of the Archaeological Evidence." *Current Anthropology* 58:S17 (2017).

Grayson, Donald K., and David J. Meltzer. "Revisiting Paleoindian Exploitation of Extinct North American Mammals." *Journal of Archaeological Science* 56 (Apr. 2015): 177–93.

Gustafson, Carl E., Richard Daugherty, and Delbert W. Gilbow. "The Manis Mastodon Site: Early Man on the Olympic Peninsula." *Canadian Journal of Archaeology* 3 (1979): 157–64.

Haile, James, Duane G. Froese, Ross D. E. MacPhee, Richard G. Roberts, Lee J. Arnold, Alberto V. Reyes, and Morten Rasmussen et al. "Ancient DNA Reveals Late Survival of Mammoth and Horse in Interior Alaska." *Proceedings of the National Academy of Sciences* 106:52 (2009): 22352–57.

Hill, Christopher, L. "Multi-Scalar Geological and Paleoenvironmental Analysis of the Lindsay Mammoth, Yellowstone Basin, Montana." Poster presented at the 2014 American Quaternary Association Conference (2014).

———. "Stratigraphic and Geochronologic Contexts of Mammoth (*Mammuthus*) and other Pleistocene Fauna, Upper Missouri Basin (Northern Great Plains and Rocky Mountains), USA." *Quaternary International* 142/143 (2006): 87–106.

———, and Leslie. B. Davis. "Stratigraphy, AMS Radiocarbon Age, and Stable Isotope Biogeochemistry of the Lindsay Mammoth, Eastern Montana." *Current Research in the Pleistocene* 15 (1998): 109–11.

Hoffecker, John. F., Scott A. Elias, Dennis H. O'Rourke, G. Richard Scott, and Nancy H. Bigelow. "Beringia and the Global Dispersal of Modern Humans." *Evolutionary Anthropology* 25:2 (Mar./Apr. 2016): 64–78.

Hofman, Jack L., Daniel S. Amick, and Richard O. Rose. "Shifting Sands: A Folsom-Midland Assemblage from a Campsite in Western Texas." *Plains Anthropologist* 35:129 (Aug. 1990): 221–53.

Holmes, Charles E. "Broken Mammoth." In *American Beginnings: The Prehistory and Paleoecology of Beringia*, edited by Frederick Hadleigh West, 312–18. Chicago: University of Chicago Press, 1996.

Hubbe, Mark, Alejandro Terrazas Mata, Brianne Herrera, Martha E. Benavente Sanvicente, Arturo González González, Carmen Rojas Sandoval, Jerónimo Avilés Olguin, Euginio Acevez Núñez, and Noreen Von Cramon-Taubadel. "Morphological Variation of the Early Human Remains from Quintana Roo, Yucatán Peninsula, Mexico: Contributions to the Discussions about the Settlement of the Americas." *PLOS ONE* 15:1 (2020): 1–22.

Ikeya, Nobuyuki. "Maritime Transport of Obsidian in Japan during the Upper Paleolithic." In *Emergence and Diversity of Modern Human Behavior in Paleolithic Asia*, edited by Yousuke Kaifu, Masami Izuho, Ted Goebel, Hiroyuki Sato, and Akira Ono, 362–72. College Station: Texas A&M University Press, 2014.

Jenkins, Dennis L., Loren G. Davis, Thomas W. Stafford Jr., Paula F. Campos, Bryan Hockett, George T. Jones, and Linda Scott Cummings et al. "Clovis Age Western Stemmed Projectile Points and Human Coprolites at the Paisley Caves." *Science* 337:6091 (Jul. 13, 2012): 223–28.

Jones, J. Scott, and Robson Bonnichsen. "The Anzick Clovis Burial." *Current Research in the Pleistocene* 11 (1994): 42–43.

Kaifu, Yousuke, Masami Izuho, Ted Goebel, Hiroyuki Sato, and Akira Ono, eds. *Emergence and Diversity of Modern Human Behavior in Paleolithic Asia*. College Station: Texas A&M University Press, 2014.

Kemp, Brian M., Ripan S. Malhi, John McDonough, Deborah A. Bolnick, Jason A. Eshleman, Olga Rickards, and Cristina Martinez-Labarga et al. "Genetic Analysis of Early Holocene Skeletal Remains from Alaska and Its Implications for the Settlement of the Americas." *American Journal of Physical Anthropology* 132:4 (Apr. 2007): 605–21.

Kilby, J. David, and Bruce Huckell. "Clovis Caches: Current Perspectives and Future Directions." In *Paleoamerican Odyssey*, edited by Kelly E. Graf, Carolyn V. Ketron, and Michael R. Waters, 257–72. College Station: Center for the Study of the First Americans, Texas A&M University, 2014.

Knudson, Ruthann. *Organizational Variability in Late Paleo-Indian Assemblages*. Washington State University Laboratory of Anthropology, Reports of Investigations no. 60. Washington State University, Pullman, 1973.

———. "We Are All One: Anzick Children Reburied." *Mammoth Trumpet* 30:2 (2015): 11–14, 20.

Kooyman, B., L. V. Hills, P. McNeil, and S. Tolman. "Late Pleistocene Horse Hunting at the Wally's Beach Site (DhPg-8), Canada." *American Antiquity* 71:1 (Jan. 2006): 101–21.

Kornfeld, Marcel, George C. Frison, and Mary L. Larson. *Prehistoric Hunter-Gatherers of the High Plains and Rockies*. London: Altamira Press, 2009.

Krasinski, Kathryn E. *Broken Bones and Cutmarks: Taphonomic Analyses and Implications for the Peopling of the Americas*. PhD dissertation, University of Nevada, Reno, 2010.

Lahren, Larry. *Homeland: An Archaeologist's View of Yellowstone Country's Past*. Livingston, MT: Cayuse Press, 2006.

———, and Robson Bonnichsen. "Bone Foreshafts from a Clovis Burial in Southwestern Montana." *Science* 186:4159 (Oct. 11, 1974): 147–50.

Lanoe, F. B., and C. E. Holmes. "Animals as Raw Material in Beringia: Insights from the Site of Swan Point CZ4B, Alaska." *American Antiquity* 81:4 (Oct. 2016): 682–96.

Lee, Craig M., Robert L. Kelly, Rachel Reckin, Ira L. Matt, and Pei-Lin Yu. "Ice Patch Archaeology in Western North America." *SAA Archaeological Record* 14 (2014): 15–19.

Llamas, Bastien, Lars Fehren-Schmitz, Guido Valverde, Julien Soubrier, Swapan Mallick, Nadin Rohland, and Susanne Nordenfelt et al. "Ancient Mitochondrial DNA Provides High-Resolution Time Scale of the Peopling of the Americas." *Science Advances* 2:4 (Apr. 1, 2016): 1–10.

Lvova, Liudmila. "The Siberian Paleolithic Site of Mal'ta: A Unique Source for the Study of Childhood Archaeology." *Evolutionary Human Sciences* 3 (2021): 1–11.

MacDonald, Douglas H. *Before Yellowstone: Native American Archaeology in the National Park*. Seattle: University of Washington Press, 2018.

———. "Modeling Folsom Mobility, Mating Strategies, and Technological Organization in the Northern Plains." *Plains Anthropologist* 44:168 (May 1999): 141–61.

———. *Montana Before History: 11,000 Years of Hunter-Gatherers in the Plains and Rockies*. Missoula, MT: Mountain Press Publishing Company, 2012.

——, Jordan C. McIntyre, and Michael C. Livers. "Understanding the Role of Yellowstone Lake in the Prehistory of Interior Northwestern North America." *North American Archaeologist* 33:3 (2012): 251–89.

——, and Matthew R. Nelson. "Paleoindians of Yellowstone Lake: Interpreting Late Pleistocene-Early Holocene Hunter-Gatherer Land-Use in the Greater Yellowstone Ecosystem." *Plains Anthropologist* 64:249 (May 2018): 1–28.

Martin, Paul S. "The Discovery of America: The First Americans May Have Swept the Western Hemisphere and Decimated Its Fauna Within 1000 Years." *Science* 179:4077 (Mar. 9, 1973): 969–74.

McLaren, Duncan, Daryl Fedje, Angela Dyck, Quentin Mackie, Alisha Gauvreau, and Jenny Cohen. "Terminal Pleistocene Epoch Human Footprints from the Pacific Coast of Canada." *PLOS ONE* 13:3 (2018):1–30.

Meltzer, David J. *First Peoples in a New World*. Berkeley: University of California Press, 2010.

——. "Pleistocene Overkill and North American Mammalian Extinctions." *Annual Review of Anthropology* 44 (2015): 33–53.

Moreno-Mayar, J. Víctor, Ben A. Potter, Lasse Vinner, Matthias Steinrücken, Simon Rasmussen, and Jonathan Terhorst et al. "Terminal Pleistocene Alaskan Genome Reveals First Founding Population of Native Americans." *Nature* 553:7687 (Jan. 11, 2018): 203–7.

Morlan, Robert E., and Jacques Cinq-Mars. "Ancient Beringians: Human Occupation in the Late Pleistocene of Alaska and the Yukon Territory." In *Paleoecology of Beringia*, edited by David M. Hopkins, John V. Matthews, Charles E. Schweger, and Steven B. Young, 353–81. New York: Academic Press, 1982.

Morrow, Juliet E., and Stuart J. Fiedel. "New Radiocarbon Dates for the Clovis Component of the Anzick Site, Park County, Montana." In *Paleoindian Archaeology: A Hemispheric Perspective*, edited by Juliet E. Morrow and Cristóbal Gnecco, 123–38. Gainesville: University Press of Florida, 2006.

Osborn, Alan J. "Eye of the Needle: Cold Stress, Clothing, and Sewing Technology During the Younger Dryas Cold Event in North America." *American Antiquity* 79:1 (Jan. 2014): 45–68.

Oviatt, Charles G., David B. Madsen, David Rhode, and Loren Davis. "A Critical Assessment of Claims that Human Footprints in the Lake Otero Basin, New Mexico Date to the Last Glacial Maximum. *Quaternary Research* 111 (Jan. 2023): 138–47.

Owsley, Douglas W., and David R. Hunt. "Clovis and Early Archaic Crania from the Anzick Site (24PA506), Park County, Montana." *Plains Anthropologist* 46:176 (May 2001): 115–24.

Palacios, David, Chris R. Stokes, Fred M. Phillips, John J. Clague, Jesus Alcalá-Reygosa, Nuria Andrés, and Isandra Angel et al. "The Deglaciation of the Americas during the Last Glacial Termination." *Earth-Science Reviews* 203 (Apr. 2020): 103–13.

Parker, John L. *Once a Runner*. New York: Scribner Publishing, 2009.

Pitulko, Vladimir V., P. A. Nikolsky, E. Y. Girya, A. E. Basilyan, V. E. Tumskoy, S. A. Koulakov, and M. A. Anisimov. "The Yana RHS Site: Humans in the Arctic Before the Last Glacial Maximum." *Science* 303:5654 (Jan. 2, 2004): 52–56.

——, Elena Y. Pavlova, and Pavel A. Nikolskiy. "Mammoth Ivory Technologies in the Upper Paleolithic: A Case Study Based on the Materials from Yana RHS, Northern Yana-Indighirka Lowland, Arctic Siberia." *World Archaeology* 47:3 (2015): 333–89.

Potter, Ben A., Joel D. Irish, Joshua D. Reuthera, and Holly J. McKinney. "New Insights into Eastern Beringian Mortuary Behavior: A Terminal Pleistocene Double Infant." *Proceedings of the National Academy of Science* 111:48 (2014): 17060–65.

——, J. D. Reuther, V. T. Holliday, C. E. Holmes, D. S. Miller, and N. Schmuck. "Early Colonization of Beringia and Northern North America: Chronology, Routes, and Adaptive Strategies." *Quaternary International* 444, part B (2017): 36–55.

Raff, Jennifer A. *Origin: A Genetic History of the Americas.* New York: Twelve Press, 2022.

——, and Deborah A. Bolnick. "Palaeogenomics: Genetic Roots of the First Americans." *Nature* 506:7487 (Feb. 12, 2014): 162–63.

Raghavan, Maanasa, Pontus Skoglund, Kelly E. Graf, Mait Metspalu, Anders Albrechtsen, Ida Moltke, and Simon Rasmussen et al. "Upper Palaeolithic Siberian Genome Reveals Dual Ancestry of Native Americans." *Nature* 505:7481 (Jan. 2, 2014): 87–91.

——, Matthias Steinrücken, Kelley Harris, Stephan Schiffels, Simon Rasmussen, Michael Degiorgio, and Anders Albrechtsen et al. "Genomic Evidence for the Pleistocene and Recent Population History of Native Americans." *Science* 349:6250 (Jul. 23, 2015): 841.

Rasmussen, Morten, Sarah L. Anzick, Michael R. Waters, Pontus Skoglund, Michael DeGiorgio, Thomas W. Stafford Jr., and Simon Rasmussen et al. "The Genome of a Late Pleistocene Human from a Clovis Burial in Western Montana." *Nature* 506:7487 (Feb. 13, 2014): 225–29

Sanchez, Guadalupe, Vance T. Holliday, Edmund P. Gaines, and Ismael Sanchez-Morales. "Human (Clovis)-Gomphothere (Cuvieronius sp.) Association ~13,390 Calibrated yBP in Sonora, Mexico." *Proceedings of the National Academy of Sciences* 111:30 (2014): 10972–77.

Sikora, Martin, Vladimir V. Pitulko, Vitor C. Sousa, Morten E. Allentoft, Lasse Vinner, Simon Rasmussen, and Ashot Margaryan et al. "The Population History of Northeastern Siberia since the Pleistocene." *Nature* 570:7760 (Jun. 13, 2019): 182–88.

Smith, Heather L., Susan C. Kuzminsky, and Anna Linderholm. "Discerning Dispersals along the Pacific and Interior Corridors: Contributions of Geometric Morphometrics to the Peopling of the Americas." *PaleoAmerica* 6:1 (2019): 1–22.

Stanford, Dennis J., and Bruce A. Bradley. *Across Atlantic Ice: The Origin of America's Clovis Culture.* Berkeley: University of California Press, 2012.

Surovell, Todd A., Vance T. Holliday, Joseph A. M. Gingerich, Caroline Ketron, C. Vance Haynes Jr., Ilene Hilman, Daniel P. Wagner, Eileen Johnson, and Philippe Claeys. "An Independent Evaluation of the Younger Dryas Extraterrestrial Impact Hypothesis." *Proceedings of the National Academy of Sciences* 106:43 (2009): 18155–58.

———, Spencer R. Pelton, Richard Anderson-Sprecher, and Adam D. Myers. "Test of Martin's Overkill Hypothesis Using Radiocarbon Dates on Extinct Megafauna." *Proceedings of the National Academy of Sciences* 113:4 (2016): 886–91.

Suttles, Wayne, ed. *Handbook of North American Indians*. Vol. 7: *Northwest Coast*. Washington DC: Smithsonian Institution, 1990.

Sutton, Mark Q. "Paleoindian-Era Osseous Rods: Distribution, Dating, and Function." *Paleoamerica* 4:3 (2018): 183–201.

Svoboda, Jiří, Miroslav Králík, Věra Čulíková, Šárka Hladilová, Martin Novák, Miriam Nývltová Fišáková, Daniel Nývlt, and Michaela Zelinková. "Pavlov VI: An Upper Palaeolithic Living Unit." *Antiquity* 83:320 (Jun. 2009): 282–95

Tamm, Erika, Toomas Kivisild, Maere Reidla, Mait Metspalu, David Glenn Smith, Connie J. Mulligan, and Claudio M. Bravi et al. "Beringian Standstill and Spread of Native American Founders." *PLOS ONE* 2:9 (2007): 829.

Vachula, Richard S., Yongsong Huang, William M. Longo, Slyvia G. Dee, William C. Daniels, and James M. Russell. "Evidence of Ice Age Humans in Eastern Beringia Suggests Early Migration to North America." *Quaternary Science Review* 205 (Feb. 1, 2019): 35–44.

Walker, James W. P., and David T. G. Clinnick. "Ten Years of Solutreans on the Ice: A Consideration of Technological Logistics and Paleogenetics for Assessing the Colonization of the Americas." *World Archaeology* 46:5 (2014): 734–51.

Waters, Michael R., Charlotte D. Pevny, and David L. Carlson. *Clovis Lithic Technology: Investigation of a Stratified Workshop at the Gault Site, Texas*. College Station: Texas A&M University Press, 2011.

———, and Thomas W. Stafford Jr. "Redefining the Age of Clovis: Implications for the Peopling of North America." *Science* 315:5815 (Feb. 23, 2007): 1122–26.

———, Thomas W. Stafford Jr., Brian Kooyman, and L. V. Hills. "Late Pleistocene Horse and Camel Hunting at the Southern Margin of the Ice-Free Corridor: Reassessing the Age of Wally's Beach, Canada." *Proceedings of the National Academy of Science* 112:14 (2015): 4263–67.

———, Thomas W. Stafford Jr., H. Gregory McDonald, Carl Gustafson, Morten Rasmussen, Enrico Cappellini, and Jesper V. Olsen et al. "Pre-Clovis Mastodon Hunting 13,800 Years Ago at the Manis Site, Washington." *Science* 334:6054 (Oct. 21, 2011): 351–53.

West, F. H. *American Beginnings: The Prehistory and Palaeoecology of Beringia*. Chicago: University of Chicago Press, 1996.

White, Samuel S. "The Anzick Artifacts: A High Technology Forager Tool Assemblage." PhD dissertation, University of Montana, Missoula, 2019.

Wilke, Philip J., J. Jeffrey Flenniken, and Terry L. Ozbun. "Clovis Technology at the Anzick Site, Montana." *Journal of California and Great Basin Anthropology* 13:2 (1991): 242–72.

Wilson, Michael Clayton, and James Burns. "Searching for the Earliest Canadians: Wide Corridors, Narrow Doorways, Small Windows." In *Ice Age People of North America: Environments, Origins, and Adaptations*, edited by R. Bonnichsen and K. L. Turnmire, 213–48. Corvallis: Oregon State University Press for the Center for the Study of the First Americans, 1999.

Wissler, Clark, and D. C. Duvall. *Mythology of the Blackfoot Indians*. 1908; reprint, Lincoln, NE: Bison Books, 2008.

Wygal, Brian T., Kathryn E. Krasinski, Charles E. Holmes, Barbara A. Crass, and Kathryn M. Smith. "Mammoth Ivory Rods in Eastern Beringia: Earliest in North America." *American Antiquity* 87:1 (2022): 59–79.

INDEX

Page numbers in *italics* refer to illustrations.